# Congressional Protection of Religious Liberty

# CONGRESSIONAL PROTECTION OF RELIGIOUS LIBERTY

LOUIS FISHER

**Novinka Books**
*New York*

**Senior Editors:** Susan Boriotti and Donna Dennis
**Coordinating Editor:** Tatiana Shohov
**Office Manager:** Annette Hellinger
**Graphics:** Wanda Serrano
**Editorial Production:** Vladimir Klestov, Matthew Kozlowski, Tom Moceri,
　　　　　　　　　　　Anthony T. Sovik and Maya Columbus
**Circulation:** Ave Maria Gonzalez, Vera Popovic, Luis Aviles, Raymond Davis,
　　　　　　　Melissa Diaz and Jeannie Pappas
**Marketing:** Cathy DeGregory

*Library of Congress Cataloging-in-Publication Data*
*Available Upon Request*

ISBN: 1-59033-669-0.

Copyright © 2003 by Novinka Books, An Imprint of
　　　　　　　Nova Science Publishers, Inc.
　　　　　　　400 Oser Ave, Suite 1600
　　　　　　　Hauppauge, New York 11788-3619
　　　　　　　Tele. 631-231-7269　　Fax 631-231-8175
　　　　　　　e-mail: Novascience@earthlink.net
　　　　　　　Web Site: http://www.novapublishers.com

All rights reserved. No part of this book may be reproduced, stored in a retrieval system or transmitted in any form or by any means: electronic, electrostatic, magnetic, tape, mechanical photocopying, recording or otherwise without permission from the publishers.

The authors and publisher have taken care in preparation of this book, but make no expressed or implied warranty of any kind and assume no responsibility for any errors or omissions. No liability is assumed for incidental or consequential damages in connection with or arising out of information contained in this book.

This publication is designed to provide accurate and authoritative information with regard to the subject matter covered herein. It is sold with the clear understanding that the publisher is not engaged in rendering legal or any other professional services. If legal or any other expert assistance is required, the services of a competent person should be sought. FROM A DECLARATION OF PARTICIPANTS JOINTLY ADOPTED BY A COMMITTEE OF THE AMERICAN BAR ASSOCIATION AND A COMMITTEE OF PUBLISHERS.

*Printed in the United States of America*

# CONTENTS

| | | |
|---|---|---|
| **Preface** | | vii |
| **Chapter 1** | Introduction | 1 |
| **Chapter 2** | Protecting Minority Rights | 3 |
| **Chapter 3** | Conscientious Objectors | 11 |
| **Chapter 4** | Compulsory Flag Salutes | 21 |
| **Chapter 5** | Religious Apparel in the Military | 27 |
| **Chapter 6** | School Prayer | 33 |
| **Chapter 7** | American Indian Religious Freedom | 41 |
| **Chapter 8** | Religious Use of Peyote | 51 |
| **Chapter 9** | Statutory Exemptions | 65 |
| **Chapter 10** | Conclusions | 75 |
| **Index** | | 77 |

# PREFACE

It is widely believed that religious liberty is mainly protected by the independent judiciary, especially for religious denominations that represent a small minority. The view is that legislative bodies — operating by majority vote — cannot be expected to protect minority rights, and that judges have the independence and technical expertise to defend the constitutional rights of minorities.

However, legislatures — at both the state and national level — have done much to protect religious liberty, including the views of religious minorities. Prior to *Cantwell* v. *Connecticut*, 310 U.S. 296 (1940), the Supreme Court had barely begun to sketch out a jurisprudence of religious freedom. For the previous century and a half, the task of protecting religious liberties fell essentially to the regular political process.

Even during the past half century, when the judicial record has measurably improved, individuals and private organizations often turn to elected officials for relief, particularly after being rebuffed by the courts. Under these pressures, it is not unusual for Congress to advance religious liberty beyond what is available from the judiciary.

This book explains how elected officials, especially Members of Congress, have protected religious liberty. To the extent that some of these statutes protect particular religious organizations (including Quakers, Mennonites, Amish, and the Native American Church), the report challenges the general view that government "may not exempt religious adherents from obligations by which nonadherents must abide; instead, exemptions from otherwise generally applicable prohibitions must be drawn on a religion-neutral basis in order to pass muster under the Establishment Clause."[1]

---

[1] U.S. Department of Justice, Office of Legislative Affairs, letter of September 25, 1998, from Acting Assistant Attorney General L. Anthony Sutin to Senator Arlen Specter, at 2.

The examples discussed in this report start with the statutory recognition of the rights of conscientious objectors and moves to more recent disputes, including compulsory flag-salutes, religious apparel in the military, school prayer, Indian religious beliefs, the religious use of peyote, and various statutory exemptions adopted by Congress and state legislatures to give protection to religious liberty.

*Chapter 1*

# INTRODUCTION

There is a belief that courts, not the political process, are the essential protectors of individual rights and religious liberties. Are legislative bodies, operating by majority vote, necessarily insensitive to minority interests? The record in the United States demonstrates that blacks, women, and other minorities often turn to elected officials for relief, sometimes after losing in the courts.

With regard to religious liberty, the origin and growth of an individual's right to believe or not believe, and the safeguarding of that right, have occurred almost entirely outside the courtroom. The regular political process has protected the religious freedom of minorities as well as — and often better than — the courts. It is often the case that action through the legislature, at both the national and the state level, supplies a breadth of religious freedom that is more generous than can be obtained from the judiciary.

Before turning to the specific issue of religious liberty, this report first examines the general question of how political institutions in America have protected minority rights. Courts were expected to have a special role in guarding individual and minority rights, but that duty has been spread more broadly, to include not just the judiciary but the legislative and executive branches as well.

*Chapter 2*

# PROTECTING MINORITY RIGHTS

In advocating the addition of a Bill of Rights to the Constitution, James Madison predicted that "independent tribunals of justice will consider themselves in a peculiar manner the guardian of those rights."[1] Nevertheless, for the first century and a half under the Constitution, individual rights were decided largely by the regular political process. When these issues were litigated and brought before federal courts, the general pattern was for judges to protect the interests of government and corporations rather than individuals and minorities.[2]

Over the past half century, courts have been more active in protecting individual and minority rights. Still, on many occasions litigants fail to receive the protections they seek in court and turn for assistance to elected officials. Through this dialogue, a majoritarian process may advances religious liberties and other rights beyond what was available in the courts. Specific examples will be discussed in this report.

Before turning to these struggles over religious liberty, it would be helpful to create a broader framework to see how the political process has protected the rights of two minorities: blacks and women.

It is fairly typical today to regard the Supreme Court as the chief protector of the rights of black citizens because of its decision in *Brown* v. *Board of Education* (1954) to strike down segregation in the schools. However, the record of the Court in the nineteenth century was quite hostile to blacks.

---

[1] 1 Annals of Cong. 439 (1789).
[2] Henry W. Edgerton, "The Incidence of Judicial Control over Congress," 22 Corn. L. Q. 299 (1937).

Opposition to slavery in the United States arose from the general public. Individual Americans came to regard slavery as repugnant to fundamental political and legal principles, especially those embedded in the Declaration of Independence. The pathbreaking antislavery documents were private writings and speeches, not court or even legislative actions.[3]

After his election as President in 1856, James Buchanan brought up the slavery issue in his inaugural address on March 4, 1857. The dispute over slavery in the territories, he said, "is a judicial question, which legitimately belongs to the Supreme Court of the United States, before whom it is now pending, and will, it is understood, be speedily and finally settled. To their decision, in common with all citizens, I shall cheerfully submit, whatever this may be."[4]

Two days later the Court issued its decision in *Dred Scott v. Sandford*, holding that black slaves and their descendants were not citizens of the United States, could not sue in court, and Congress lacked constitutional power to prevent the spread of slavery to the territories in the West. Unlike Buchanan's willingness to accept whatever the Court decided, citizens took sides.

In the historic debates between Senator Stephen A. Douglas and Abraham Lincoln, Lincoln accepted the decision as it applied to Dred Scott but rejected the rulings on citizenship and slavery in the territories as a nullity, to be left to political resolution outside the courts.[5] In his inaugural address in 1861, he denied that constitutional questions could be settled solely by the Court. If government policy on "vital questions affecting the whole people is to be irrevocably fixed" by the Court, "the people will have ceased to be their own rulers, having to that extent practically resigned their Government into the hands of that eminent tribunal."[6]

*Dred Scott* was eventually overturned by the Thirteenth, Fourteenth, and Fifteenth Amendments, which were ratified from 1865 to 1870, but before action on those amendments Congress and the President had already taken steps to repudiate the main tenets of that decision. Congress passed legislation in 1862 to prohibit slavery in the territories.[7] During debate on

---

[3] William M. Wiecek, The Sources of Antislavery Constitutionalism in America, 1760-1848 (1977).
[4] 7 The Messages and Papers of the Presidents 2962 (James D. Richardson ed. 1897) (hereafter "Richardson").
[5] 2 Collected Works of Abraham Lincoln 516 (Roy P. Easler ed. 1953).
[6] Id. at 520.
[7] 12 Stat. 432, c. 111 (1862).

this bill, lawmakers did not even mention the Court's decision.[8] They never doubted their constitutional power to prohibit slavery in the territories. Also in 1862, Attorney General Edward Bates released a detailed opinion in which he held that neither color nor race could deny American blacks the right of citizenship. He denied that *Dred Scott* determined the question of blacks to be citizens, regarding language from Chief Justice Taney as pure dicta and "of no authority as a judicial decision."[9]

After the Civil War, Congress passed a number of statutes to protect the rights of blacks, but many of these statutes were either nullified by the Court or weakened through judicial interpretation. In 1866, Congress passed the Civil Rights Act to extend to blacks the same legal rights enjoyed by whites.[10] President Andrew Johnson vetoed the bill, claiming that it invaded the rights of the states, but Congress overrode the veto.[11] The Court proceeded to water down the statute with narrow, technical decisions.[12]

In 1875, Congress passed legislation that gave blacks equal access to public accommodations, such as inns, "conveyances" (transportation), theaters, and other places of public amusement. The statute attempted to close the gap between the Declaration of Independence and the Constitution by stating, in the preamble, "Whereas, it is essential to just government we recognize the equality of all men before the law."[13] However, the Court in 1883 invalidated the statute as a federal encroachment on the states and an interference with private relationships.[14] As a result of the Court's action, what could have been accomplished in 1875 had to await the Civil Rights Act of 1964, finally giving blacks equal access to public accommodations. By the end of the nineteenth century, congressional interest in civil rights had lost its momentum.

Just as Congress tried to protect the rights of blacks during the decades after the Civil War, so did it enact legislation to protect the rights of women to practice law. Victories that women gained during this time came mainly from legislative action. In 1869, the Supreme Court of Illinois held that Myra Bradwell could not be admitted to practice law in the state. Of her qualifications the Court had "no doubt."[15] However, the decision advised

---

[8] Cong. Globe, 37th Cong., 2d Sess. 2030, 2041-54, 2061-64, 2066-69, 2618, 2624, 2769 (1862).
[9] 10 Ops. Att'y Gen. 382, 412 (1862).
[10] 14 Stat. 27 (1866).
[11] 8 Richardson 3604.
[12] For example, Blyew v. United States, 80 U.S. (13 Wall.) 581 (1872).
[13] 18 Stat. 335 (1875).
[14] The Civil Rights Cases, 109 U.S. 3 (1883).
[15] In re Bradwell, 55 Ill. 535, 536 (1869).

her, or any other interested person, to present the issue to the state legislature for relief. If changes needed to be made in the legal position of women, "let it be made by that department of the government to which the constitution has entrusted the power of changing the laws."[16] The Illinois legislature passed a law in 1872, stating "that no person shall be precluded or debarred from any occupation, profession or employment (except military) on account of sex: *Provided*, that this act shall not be construed to affect the eligibility of any person to an elective office."[17]

Having prevailed at the state level, Myra Bradwell appealed her case to the U.S. Supreme Court to establish a national right. She argued that her right to practice law was protected by the Fourteenth Amendment guarantee of privileges and immunities, but the Court held against her.[18] She then went to Congress, asking it to remove the legal disabilities that prevented women from practicing law. The House of Representatives, voting 169 to 87, passed legislation in 1878 to provide that any woman who was a member of the bar of the highest court of any state or territory or of the Supreme Court of the District of Columbia for at least three years, maintained a good standing before such court, and was a person of good moral character, should be admitted to practice before the U.S. Supreme Court.[19]

Senator George Hoar rejected the argument that the Court should be left alone to decide by its own rules who may practice before it: "Now, with the greatest respect for that tribunal, I conceive that the law-making and not the law-expounding power in this Government ought to determine the question what class of citizens shall be clothed with the office of the advocate."[20] The bill passed the Senate, 39 to 20. Thus, an all-male legislative body provided impressive support to women's rights — rights that were unavailable from the Supreme Court.[21]

It might be argued that Congress during the period after the Civil War acted against the rights of minorities, such as the legislation passed to prohibit polygamy by Mormons. Was this an infringement of religious liberty? Congress passed legislation in 1862 to prohibit polygamy. When the Mormon Church refused to comply with the statute, Congress resorted to other sanctions in 1882: making polygamists ineligible to serve on juries, to

---

[16] Id. at 540.
[17] 1872 Illinois Laws 578 (March 22, 1872).
[18] Bradwell v. State, 83 U.S. (16 Wall.) 130 (1873).
[19] 7 Cong. Rec. 1235 (1878).
[20] 8 Cong. Rec. 1084 (1879).
[21] 20 Stat. 292, ch. 81 (1879).

vote, or to hold territorial or federal office. Finally, in 1887, Congress passed legislation to confiscate Church property.[22]

However, these statutes respected constitutional principles by taking aim at religious practices, not religious beliefs. The prohibition on polygamy did not interfere with the right "to worship God according to the dictates of conscience."[23] The Court upheld the statutory prohibition by drawing the same distinction between belief and practice: "Laws are made for the government of actions, and while they cannot interfere with mere religious belief and opinions, they may with practices."[24]

The 1882 statute explained that voting rights were being denied to those who practiced polygamy, bigamy, or cohabitation, not to those who entertained an "opinion" on the subject.[25] The Court upheld this statute.[26] When Congress passed the bill to confiscate Mormon Church property, Senator George Edmunds emphasized that the bill "deals with conduct and states of fact, not opinions, faiths, or beliefs."[27] In upholding this statute, the Court dismissed the argument that the practice of polygamy constituted "a religious belief" to be protected by the Constitution.[28]

Following this last opinion, the President of the Mormon Church issued a proclamation against polygamy, stating that he would submit to federal law.[29] In 1894, Congress passed legislation enabling the people of Utah to form a constitution and be admitted as a state. Congress set forth these distinctions between religious beliefs and religious practices: "That perfect toleration of religious sentiment shall be secured, and that no inhabitant of said State shall ever be molested in person or property on account of his or her mode of religious worship: *Provided*, That polygamous or plural marriages are forever prohibited."[30] Those principles were repeated two years later when President Grover Cleveland proclaimed that Utah had been admitted to the Union.[31]

Despite the modest record of the Supreme Court in protecting the rights of minorities, it was at times singled out as the guardian of individual rights.

---

[22] 12 Stat. 501 (1862); 22 Stat. 30 (1882); 24 Stat. 637, § 13 (1887).
[23] 12 Stat. 501, § 2 (1862).
[24] Reynolds v. United States, 98 U.S. 145, 166 (1879).
[25] 22 Stat. 30, 32, § 9 (1882).
[26] Murphy v. Ramsey, 114 U.S. 15 (1885).
[27] 17 Cong. Rec. 407 (1886).
[28] Mormon Church v. United States, 136 U.S. 1, 49 (1890).
[29] 2 Anson Phelps Stokes, Church and State in the United States 280 (1950) (hereafter "Stokes"); Orma Linford, "The Mormons and the Law: The Polygamy Cases" (Part II), 9 Utah L. Rev. 543, 582-83 (1965).
[30] 28 Stat. 108, § 3 (1894).
[31] 29 Stat. 876 (1896).

In 1937, when the Senate Judiciary Committee repudiated President Franklin D. Roosevelt's court-packing plan, the committee report claimed the minority political groups "no less than religious and racial groups, have never failed, when forced to appeal to the Supreme Court of the United States, to find in its opinions the reassurance and protection of their constitutional rights."[32] The committee said that the framers "never wavered in their belief that an independent judiciary and a Constitution defining with clarity the rights of the people, were the only safeguards of the citizen."[33] That may have been the framers' hope, but the judicial record fell far short of that standard.

At the time of the Senate's consideration of the court-packing bill, Henry W. Edgerton, who later become a federal judge, had completed an analysis of the extent to which judicial review had been used to protect individual liberties, especially those of "relatively poor and unprivileged majority on the one hand, or of a relatively well-to-do minority on the other hand."[34] In the entire list of Supreme Court decisions from 1789 to 1937, Edgerton could not find a single one that protected the civil liberties of speech, press, or assembly. Instead, he concluded that the Court regularly protected the interests of government and corporations.

A few years after Edgerton's study, Henry Steele Commager concluded that the Court had "intervened again and again to defeat congressional efforts to free slaves, guarantee civil rights to Negroes, to protect workingmen, outlaw child labor, assist hard-pressed farmers, and to democratize the tax system."[35] In response to this judicial record, Justice Oliver Wendell Holmes, Jr. remarked: "It must be remembered that legislatures are ultimate guardians of the liberties and welfare of the people in quite as great a degree as the courts."[36]

The desegregation decision of 1954 probably represents, in the minds of many, the clearest example of the Court protecting minority rights. In important ways, *Brown* v. *Board of Education* aroused the public conscience and articulated newly-defined constitutional values.[37] That decision by itself, however, had little direct impact on integrating schools. As late as 1964, the Court complained that there "has been entirely too much deliberation and not

---

[32] S. Rept. No. 711, 75th Cong., 1st Sess. 20 (1937).
[33] Id. at 19.
[34] Henry W. Edgerton, "The Incidence of Judicial Control over Congress," 22 Corn. L. Q. 299, 301 (1937).
[35] Henry Steele Commager, Majority Rule and Minority Rights 55 (1943).
[36] Missouri, Kansas & Texas Ry. Co. v. May, 194 U.S. 267, 270 (1904).
[37] 347 U.S. 483 (1954).

enough speed" in enforcing Brown.[38] A federal appellate court in 1966 remarked: "A national effort, bringing together Congress, the executive and the judiciary may be able to make meaningful the right of Negro children to equal educational opportunities. *The courts acting alone have failed.*"[39] What finally made a difference was a series of congressional enactments: the Civil Rights Act of 1964, the Voting Rights Act of 1965, and the Fair Housing Act of 1968, all of which were upheld by the Court.

The movement for women's rights in the twentieth century came largely from legislatures. It was not until 1971 that the Supreme Court decided a case that struck down sex discrimination.[40] The judicial record prior to that was so bleak that one study concluded that "by and large the performance of American judges in the area of sex discrimination can be succinctly described as ranging from poor to abominable."[41]

This pattern of the rights of blacks and women being protected outside the courts applies equally well to religious liberty. Matters of religious conviction come first from individuals and religious groups. Their beliefs are protected largely by elected officials and the political process. This general point can be demonstrated by looking at some specific areas of religious struggle.

---

[38] Griffin v. School Bd., 377 U.S. 218, 229 (1964).
[39] United States v. Jefferson County Board of Education, 372 F.2d 836, 847 (5th Cir. 1966 (emphasis in original).
[40] Reed v. Reed, 404 U.S. 71 (1971) (voiding an Idaho law that preferred men over women in administering estates).
[41] John D. Johnston, Jr. & Charles L. Knapp, "Sex Discrimination by Law: A Study in Judicial Perspective," 46 N.Y.U. L. Rev. 675, 676 (1971).

*Chapter 3*

# CONSCIENTIOUS OBJECTORS

The first governmental institution in the United States to recognize the rights of conscientious objectors was the legislature. Under pressure from religious organizations and other groups, lawmakers carved out exemptions for those who refused to bear arms for religious or ethical reasons. Presidents and executive officials have played important roles in protecting conscientious objectors, as have the states.

In requiring citizens to serve in the militia, American colonies and early state governments made exceptions for individuals who presented religious objections. Massachusetts (1661), Rhode Island (1673), and Pennsylvania (1757) passed legislation to allow conscientious objectors to perform noncombatant services. For example, the Pennsylvania law provided that all "Quakers, Mennonists, Moravians, and others conscientiously scrupulous of bearing arms" were entitled, upon the call to arms, to assist by extinguishing fires, suppressing the insurrection of slaves and other persons, caring for the wounded, and performing other services.[1]

On July 18,1775, the Continental Congress debated plans to put the militia "into a proper state of defence." It recommended that all able-bodied men, between sixteen and fifty years of age, form themselves into regular companies of militia. The Congress also announced: "As there are some people, who, from religious principles, cannot bear arms in any case, this Congress intend no violence to their consciences, but earnestly recommend it to them, to contribute liberally in this time of universal calamity, to the relief of their distressed brethren in the several colonies, and to do all other

---

[1] U.S. Selective Service System, Conscientious Objection (Special Monograph No. 11, Vol. I) 30 (1950).

services to their oppressed Country, which they can consistently with their religious principles."[2]

After the Declaration of Independence, a number of state constitutions specifically recognized the rights of conscientious objectors. The 1776 Pennsylvania constitution provided: "Nor can any man who is conscientiously scrupulous of bearing arms, be justly compelled thereto, if he will pay such equivalent."[3] The Vermont Constitution of 1777 stated that no one "conscientiously scrupulous of bearing arms, [may] be justly compelled thereto."[4] The New Hampshire Constitution of 1784 contained language similar to Pennsylvania's.[5] The Maine Constitution of 1819 identified the religious sects entitled to exemption: "Persons of the denomination of Quakers and Shakers... may be exempted from military duty; but no other person... shall be so exempted, unless he shall pay an equivalent, to be fixed by law."[6]

The issue of conscientious objection was also considered by the First Congress. In the House of Representatives, James Madison submitted a list of amendments to the Constitution, which formed the basis for the Bill of Rights. Among his recommendations was this language: "The right of the people to keep and bear arms shall not be infringed; a well armed and well regulated militia being the best security of a free country: but no person religiously scrupulous of bearing arms shall be compelled to render military service in person."[7] Some members opposed the exception, fearing that too many people would claim conscientious objection. Rep. Elbridge Gerry of Massachusetts wanted the language limited to individuals belonging to a "religious sect scrupulous of bearing arms." Rep. James Jackson thought that Gerry exaggerated the danger, but suggested this final clause: "upon paying an equivalent, to be established by law."[8]

After further debate, the House accepted this language: "A well regulated militia, composed of the body of the people, being the best security of a free state, the right of the people to keep and bear arms, shall not be infringed, but no one religiously scrupulous of bearing arms shall be compelled to render military service in person."[9] However, when the Senate

---

[2] 2 Journals of the Continental Congress 189 (1905).
[3] Pa. Const, of 1776, VIII; 8 Sources and Documents of United States Constitutions (William F. Swindler, ed., 10 vols., 1973-79) (hereafter "Swindler").
[4] Vt. Const. of 1777, Ch. I, IX; 9 Swindler 490.
[5] N.H. Const. of 1784, Art. I, XIII; 6 Swindler 345.
[6] Me. Const. of 1819, Art. VII, Sec. 5; 4 Swindler 323.
[7] 1 Annals of Cong. 434 (1789).
[8] Id. at 750.
[9] 1 Senate Journal 63-64 (1789).

acted on what would become the Second Amendment, it deleted the religious exemption.[10]

The next year, when Congress debated the militia bill, the issue of a religious exemption was raised again. On December 17, 1790, Congress received a petition from the Quakers, "praying an exemption from militia duties and penalties on that account."[11] A number of objections were offered, including the lack of a procedure for identifying the individuals who were really conscientiously scrupulous. No tribunal had been created, Rep. James Jackson noted, "to make them swear to their scruples."[12]

Unlike some other legislators, James Madison did not restrict the exemption to particular religious denominations, but placed the emphasis on conscience.[13] On December 23, he offered language providing an exemption for "all persons religiously scrupulous of bearing arms, who shall make a declaration of the same before a civil magistrate, ... but be liable to a penalty of _____ dollars."[14] On the following day, after hearing a number of objections to the language, the House eliminated the religious exemptions and left the matter to the states.[15]

Congress did not rely on conscription during the American Revolution, the War of 1812, or the Mexican War. The country depended on volunteers and state militias to do the fighting. The first national effort to draft soldiers came with the Civil War. During debate in Congress on the 1863 conscription bill, Senator Ira Harris of New York proposed that all persons "who, being from scruples of conscience averse to bearing arms, are by the constitution of any State excused therefrom."[16] Senator Henry Wilson of Massachusetts wanted the amendment modified to read "the constitution or law of any State," because some states recognized the exemption for Shakers and Quakers in law but not in the constitution. After several other Senators raised objections to the religious exemption, Harris withdrew his amendment.

In the House, a number of amendments were offered on conscientious objectors in order to validate religious claims.[17] In the end, the bill that became law made no mention of conscientious objectors.[18] Quakers and

---

[10] Id. at 71, 77.
[11] 2 Annals of Cong. 1859 (1790).
[12] Id. at 1865.
[13] Id. at 1871-72.
[14] Id. at 1874.
[15] Id. at 1875.
[16] Cong. Globe, 37th Cong., 3d Sess. 994 (1863).
[17] For details on the House debate, see Louis Fisher, Religious Liberty in America: Political Safeguards 88 (2002).
[18] 12 Stat. 731 (1863).

other individuals could avail themselves of language in the statute that allowed drafted persons to "furnish an acceptable substitute to take his place in the draft" or pay to the government a sum not exceeding $300.[19] However, Quakers argued that payment or seeking a substitute would still violate their religious belief in being opposed to war.[20] Toward the end of 1863, Secretary of War Edwin Stanton tried to devise a compromise that would satisfy both the government and the Quakers, who he knew opposed not only war but also slavery. With great ingenuity, he proposed a Special Fund for the benefit of freed slaves. Any Quaker who paid $300 into that account would be exempt from military service.[21]

Quakers met with Members of Congress to seek a legislative solution. On January 14, 1864, Senator Wilson offered an amendment to give members of "religious denominations conscientiously opposed to the bearing of arms" some options. They could be drafted as noncombatants and assigned to duty in the hospitals or to the care of freedmen, or they could pay $300 to individuals designated by the Secretary of War, to be applied to the benefit of sick and wounded soldiers.[22] As enacted on February 24, the bill provided an exemption for members of "religious denominations, who shall by oath and affirmation declare that they are conscientiously opposed to the bearing of arms, and who are prohibited from doing so by the rules and articles of faith and practice of said denominations." These individuals would be drafted into noncombatant service and assigned to duty in hospitals or to the care of freedmen. An alternative would be to pay $300, to be applied to the benefit of sick and wounded soldiers.[23]

While Quakers appreciated the motivation behind the 1864 statute, some continued to oppose any contribution to the war effort, including making payments, assisting in hospitals, or serving freedmen.[24] As a result of a House amendment sponsored by Rep. Thaddeus Stevens and a second statutory provision,[25] the Lincoln Administration "respected more and more the wishes of those conscientiously opposed to bearing arms, by not forcing them into any kind of service against their will."[26] President Lincoln, urged to force Quakers, Mennonites, and other conscientious objectors into the Army, replied: "No, I will not do that. These people do not believe in war.

---

[19] Id. at 733, § 13.
[20] Edward Needles Wright, Conscientious Objectors in the Civil War 69-70 (1931).
[21] Id. at 72.
[22] Cong. Globe, 38th Cong., 1st Sess. 204 (1864).
[23] 13 Stat. 9, § 17 (1864).
[24] Wright, Conscientious Objectors in the Civil War, at 83-84.
[25] Cong. Globe, 38th Cong., 1st Sess. 3316, 3354-55 (1864); 13 Stat. 380, § 10 (1864).
[26] Wright, Conscientious Objectors in the Civil War, at 86.

People who do not believe in war make poor soldiers. Besides, the attitude of these people has always been against slavery. If all our people held the same views about slavery as these people there would be no war.... We will leave them on their farms where they are at home, and where they will make their contribution better than they would with a gun."[27]

The conscription statutes enacted during World War I did not allow citizens to hire substitutes or pay a commutation fee. The rights of conscientious objectors were recognized from the start, with distinctions drawn between combatant and noncombatant duties. The National Defense Act of 1916 included an exemption from military service in a noncombatant capacity for all persons of religious belief "if the conscientious holding of such belief by such person shall be established under such regulations as the President shall prescribe."[28] Unlike the Civil War statutes, which limited the exemption to members of "religious denominations," the 1916 statute did not require membership in a religious group. However, legislation the next year did require membership in a religious organization. Nothing in the statute was to be construed "to require or compel any person to serve in any of the forces herein provided for who is found to be a member of any well-recognized religious sect or organization at present organized and existing and whose existing creed or principles forbid its members to participate in war in any form and whose religious convictions are against war...."[29] Legislative efforts to delete the membership requirement were unsuccessful.[30]

Selective Service regulations in 1917 stated that any registrant found by a local board to be a member of "any well-recognized religious sect or organization organized and existing May 18, 1917," and whose "then existing creed or principles" opposed war or participation in war, shall be furnished a certificate that he can be required to serve in a capacity declared by the President to be noncombatant.[31] On March 20, 1918, President Woodrow Wilson issued an executive order setting forth guidelines for the kinds of noncombatant service to be performed, including service in the Medical Corps, the Quartermaster Corps, and the engineer service. Section 3 of the order broadened the category of conscientious objector to include not

---

[27] Selective Service System, Conscientious Objection, at 42-43.
[28] 39 Stat. 197, § 59 (1916).
[29] 40 Stat. 78, § 4 (1917).
[30] 55 Cong. Rec. 1473, 1476-79, 1528-30, 1533 (1917); for details of this debate, see Fisher, Religious Liberty in America, at 92-93.
[31] Lillian Schlissel, ed., Conscience in America: A Documentary History of Conscientious Objection in America, 1757-1967, at 133 (1968).

only members of "any well-recognized religious sect or organization" but also those "who profess religious or other conscientious scruples."[32]

The 1917 draft law was challenged in court on a number of grounds, including the charge that the exemption for conscientious objectors was repugnant to the First Amendment by establishing or interfering with religion. A unanimous Court found no merit to that argument.[33]

During World War II, Congress again debated the issue of whether membership in an established church was necessary to qualify for the status of conscientious objector. More American churches supported the right of their members to object to participation in wars, church members were encouraged to follow their own consciences, and more individuals understood that they could be conscientious objectors even without membership in a religious organization.[34]

When the Selective Training and Service Act of 1940 was introduced in bill form, it limited the exemption for conscientious objectors to persons who were members "of any well recognized religious sect whose creed or principles forbid its members to participate in war in any form."[35] That phrase was lifted from the 1917 statute. A companion bill in the Senate adopted the same language.[36] As the bill moved through committee, it dropped the reference to religious organizations. For example, the reported Senate bill covered any person who by religious training and belief was conscientiously opposed to participating in war in any form.[37]

The change resulted from testimony received from religious organizations. The broader coverage was first suggested by two Quakers during House hearings and in a meeting at the War Department.[38] Raymond Wilson, a Quaker, told the House Military Committee that the statutory phrase "well-recognized religious sect" would benefit Quakers "but we do not believe that they have any right of preferential treatment. We want the consideration on the basis of conscience rather than on the basis of membership."[39] Harold Evans, representing the Religious Society of Friends, made the same point to the Senate Military Affairs Committee.[40]

---

[32] Walter Guest Kellogg, The Conscientious Objector 22 (1919).
[33] Selective Draft Law Cases, 245 U.S. 366, 389-90 (1918).
[34] 3 Stokes 293-95.
[35] H.R. 10132, 76th Cong., 3d Sess. 8 (1940).
[36] S. 4164, 76th Cong., 3d Sess. 8 (1940).
[37] S. Kept. No. 2002, 76th Cong., 3d Sess. 3 (1940).
[38] Julien Cornell, The Conscientious Objector and the Law 7, 12 (1943). See also Selective Service System, Conscientious Objection, at 70-79.
[39] National Service Board for Religious Objectors, Congress Looks at the Conscientious Objector 15 (1943). See also his testimony reproduced at 74-75.
[40] Id. at 28.

A separate issue concerned language in the bill as introduced that limited the religious exemption to members of a sect whose "creed or principles forbid its members to participate in war in any form." Several individuals testified that members of their religious group were conscientious objectors, even though the group had no creed objecting to war.[41] C. S. Longacre, representing the Seventh-Day Adventists, told the House Military Affairs Committee: "Our constitution does not recognize church creeds. It recognizes the rights of individual consciences."[42] Subsequent versions of the bill from the House committee and the conference committee retained the emphasis on individual conscience.[43]

As enacted, the 1940 legislation contains a list of exemptions, including anyone who, "by reason of religious training and belief, is conscientiously opposed to participation in war in any form." Unlike the language in the World War I statutes, it was not necessary to be a member of a religious organization. Options included noncombatant service as defined by the President. If the individual opposed noncombatant service, he could be assigned to work "of national importance under civilian direction."[44]

A Supreme Court ruling in 1946 recognized that Congress, in conscription statutes, made accommodations for citizens with religious scruples. Congress had demonstrated respect "for the conscience of those having religious scruples against bearing arms."[45]

Congress and the judiciary became involved in a different issue: Whether the conscientious objector exemption required belief in a "Supreme Being." Language in the 1940 statute led to disagreement about the meaning of "religious training and belief." General Lewis B. Hershey, Director of Selective Service, issued an opinion stating that a conscientious objector would have to recognize "some source of all existence which is divine because it is the source of all things."[46]

In lower court rulings, the Second Circuit developed a definition of religion that did not seem to require belief in a deity. It spoke about "a response of the individual to an inward mentor, call it conscience or God, that is for many people at the present time the equivalent of what has always

---

[41] Id. at 24 (Dorothy Day, editor of the *Catholic Worker*).
[42] Id. at 71.
[43] H. Rept. No. 2903, 76th Cong., 3d Sess. 5 (1940); H. Rept. No. 2937, 76th Cong., 3d Sess. 5, 17-18 (1940).
[44] 54 Stat. 889, § 5(g) (1940).
[45] Girouard v. United States, 328 U.S. 61, 66-67 (946), overruling United States v. Macintosh, 282 U.S. 605 (1931) and United States v. Bland, 283 U.S. 636 (1931).
[46] Cornell, The Conscientious Objector and the Law, at 13.

been thought a religious impulse."[47] The Ninth Circuit, however, adopted a more traditional definition of religion. Requests to be classified as a conscientious objector could not be based on philosophical, moral, or social policy "without the concept of deity."[48]

Congressional action in 1948 seemed to reflect the position of the Ninth Circuit. The religious exemption for conscientious objectors defined "religious training and belief" to mean "an individual's belief in a relation to a Supreme Being involving duties superior to those arising from any human relation, but does not include essentially political, sociological, or philosophical views or a merely personal moral code."[49] A Senate report cited the Ninth Circuit opinion, but floor debate in the House and Senate did not discuss a relationship between religious belief and a Supreme Being.[50]

In 1955, the Supreme Court dealt with two conscientious objector cases,[51] eventually leading to a case in 1965 testing the meaning of belief in "a Supreme Being." If Congress was in fact offering a legal benefit to one type of conscientious objector — those who professed belief in a Supreme Being — and that term was equivalent to God, the statute was unlikely to survive judicial scrutiny. That was particularly so after the Court, in 1961, struck down a requirement that a notary public take an oath affirming a belief in God. The Court ruled that government may not "aid those religions based on a belief in the existence of God as against those religions founded on different beliefs."[52]

Rather than strike down the statutory language about a belief in "a Supreme Being," the Court chose to define the term broadly. It said that "the test of belief 'in a relation to a Supreme Being' is whether a given belief that is sincere and meaningful occupies a place in the life of its possessor parallel to that filled by the orthodox belief in God of one who clearly qualifies for the exemption."[53] In other words, "a Supreme Being" could be some force outside oneself, even if not a traditional deity. The Court seemed to accept the Second Circuit's position (treating conscience as roughly synonymous

---

[47] United States v. Kauten, 133 F.2d 703, 708 (2d Cir. 1943). This more generous definition of religious belief also appears in other Second Circuit decisions, including United States v. Downer, 135 F.2d 521 (1943) and United States v. Badt, 141 F.2d 845 (1944).
[48] Berman v. United States, 156 F.2d 377, 381 (9th Cir. 1946), cert. denied, 329 U.S. 795 (1946).
[49] 62 Stat. 613 (1948).
[50] S. Rept. No. 1268, 80th Cong., 2d Sess. 14 (1948); 94 Cong. Rec. 7277-79, 7303-07 (1948).
[51] Witmer v. United States, 348 U.S. 375 (1955); Sicurella v. United States, 348 U.S. 385 (1955).
[52] Torcaso v. Watkins, 367 U.S. 488, 495 (1961).
[53] United States v. Seeger, 380 U.S. 163, 165-66 (1965).

with God) rather than the more restrictive definition developed by the Ninth Circuit.

In 1967, Congress revisited the issue by removing the statute's definition of religious training and belief ("an individual's belief in a relation to a Supreme Being involving duties superior to those arising from any human relation").[54] What the Court in effect deleted, Congress deleted by statute. Committee reports detail the controversies leading up to the 1965 Court decision.[55]

Public policy on conscientious objectors reflects several centuries of commitment and understanding by individuals, religious groups, and elected officials. Congress and state legislatures, not judges, created the exemption and recognized the legitimacy of individual conscience. Courts were not a part of this dialogue until recent decades, and their contribution was not in creating the exemption but rather in defining and broadening some statutory terms.

---

[54] 81 Stat. 104 (1967).
[55] H. Rept. No. 267, 90th Cong. 1st Sess. 31, 61 (1967); H. Rept. No. 346, 90th Cong., 1st Sess. 15 (1967).

*Chapter 4*

# COMPULSORY FLAG SALUTES

A decision by the Supreme Court in 1940 upheld a compulsory flag-salute over the religious objections of Jehovah's Witnesses. After criticism from newspapers, law reviews, religious organizations, states, and Congress, the Court reversed itself three years later. Through these pressures, the larger political system insisted on a policy more protective of religious liberty than had first been announced by the Court.

The first flag-salute statute appeared in Kansas in 1907. Over time, other states passed legislation to compel schoolchildren to salute the flag. Jehovah's Witnesses, relying on a literal interpretation of the Bible, believed that saluting a secular symbol violated their religious beliefs.[1] The compulsory flag salute survived a number of early test cases,[2] but in 1937 a federal district judge in Pennsylvania found this type of statute unconstitutional.[3] The case involved the refusal of two children, Lillian Gobitas (thirteen years old) and her brother William (twelve), to salute the flag because of their religious beliefs as Jehovah's Witnesses. The family name would be incorrectly spelled "Gobitis" throughout the litigation.[4]

---

[1] "Thou shalt not make unto thee any graven image, or any likeness of any thing that is in heaven above, or that is in the earth beneath, or that is in the water under the earth. Thou shalt not bow down thyself to them, nor serve them" (Exodus 20:4-5).

[2] Leoles v. Landers, 192 S.E. 218 (Ga. 1937), dismissed for want of substantial federal question, 302 U.S. 656 (1937); Hering v. State Board of Education, 189 A. 629 (N.J. 1937), dismissed for want of substantial federal question, 303 U.S. 624 (1938); Gabrielli v. Knickerbocker, 82 P.2d 391 (Cal. 1938), dismissed for want of jurisdiction, 306 U.S. 621 (1939); Johnson v. Deerfield, 25 F.Supp. 918 (D. Mass. 139), aff'd, 306 U.S. 621 (1939).

[3] Gobitis v. Minersville School Dist., 21 F.Supp. 581 (E.D. Pa. 1937).

[4] Shawn Francis Peters, Judging Jehovah's Witnesses: Religious Persecution and the Dawn of the Rights Revolution 19 (2000).

The judge in Pennsylvania ruled that if someone on the basis of sincere religious beliefs defied a statute, the individual's right would prevail unless the state demonstrated that the statute was necessary for the public safety, health, morals, property, or personal rights.[5] He appealed to the tradition in Pennsylvania to respect religious belief and individual conscience. The founder of Pennsylvania, William Penn, had been expelled from Oxford University "for his refusal for conscience' sake to comply with regulations not essentially dissimilar [to the compulsory flag salute]."[6] His decision was upheld by the Third Circuit.[7]

The Supreme Court agreed to hear the case, but before issuing a ruling it decided another Jehovah's Witness case involving the prosecution of a Witness for soliciting money and selling books without first obtaining advance approval from a public official. A unanimous Court struck down the state law as a violation of the free exercise of religion. In this same case, the Court held that the Free Exercise Clause of the First Amendment applied to the states.[8]

Two weeks later, the Court released an opinion that upheld the compulsory flag salute. Writing for an 8 to 1 majority, Justice Frankfurter leaned heavily on two premises: liberty requires unifying sentiments, and national unity promotes national security.[9] Justice Stone's dissent attacked a number of Frankfurter's arguments, especially his doctrine of judicial self-restraint. To defer to legislative judgment and the democratic process, said Stone, "seems to me no less than the surrender of the constitutional protection of the liberty of small minorities to the popular will."[10]

Frankfurter's decision was excoriated by law journals, the press, and religious organizations. The *New Republic*, which Frankfurter helped found, warned that the country was "in great danger of adopting Hitler's philosophy in the effort to oppose Hitler's legions," and accused the Court of coming "dangerously close to being a victim of [war] hysteria."[11] Thirty-one of thirty-nine law reviews that discussed the decision did so critically. Newspapers accused the Court of violating constitutional rights and buckling

---

[5] Gobitis v. Minersville School Dist., 21 F.Supp. at 584.
[6] Id. at 585.
[7] Minersville School Dist. v. Gobitis, 108 F.2d 683 (3d Cir. 1939).
[8] Cantwell v. Connecticut, 310 U.S. 296, 303 (1940).
[9] Minersville School District v. Gobitis, 310 U.S. 586 (1940).
[10] Id. at 606.
[11] "Frankfurter v. Stone," The New Republic, vol. 102, at 843-44 (June 24, 1940).

under popular hysteria.[12] Editorials in 171 newspapers condemned Frankfurter's opinion.[13]

Frankfurter's decision was followed by a wave of violence against Witnesses across the country. John Noonan writes: "Planned by no central authority, unintended by the Supreme Court, overshadowed by World War II, the legal and illegal persecution of Witnesses from 1941 to 1943 was the greatest outbreak of religious intolerance in twentieth-century America."[14] Within weeks of the decision, hundreds of attacks were reported by the Justice Department.[15]

Justices Black, Douglas, and Murphy, part of Frankfurter's 8-1 majority, soon regretted their votes. A few months after the decision, Douglas told Frankfurter that Black was having second thoughts. Sarcastically, Frankfurter asked whether Black had spent the summer reading the Constitution. "No," Douglas replied, "he has been reading the papers."[16]

Several state courts found Frankfurter's opinion unacceptable. Reliance on state constitutional law would soon provide greater protection to religious liberty than could be obtained from the U.S. Supreme Court. In New Hampshire, after the children of Jehovah's Witnesses were suspended from public school because they refused the salute the flag, and were taken from their family and placed in a state industrial school, the Supreme Court of New Hampshire deplored the breaking up of a family for "no more than the conscientious acts of the children, based upon the religious teachings of their parents."[17] Similar rulings were handed down by state courts in New Jersey, Kansas, and Washington.[18]

This nationwide debate had a profound impact on the U.S. Supreme Court. In 1942, Justices Black, Douglas, and Murphy publicly apologized for their votes in *Gobitis*. They now announced that it has been "wrongly decided."[19] Deserted by his three colleagues, Frankfurter was left with a bare 5-4 majority. The margin was even shakier because two members of the *Gobitis* majority had left the Court and been replaced by Wiley Rutledge and

---

[12] David R. Manwaring, Render Unto Caesar: The Flag-Salute Controversy 158-60 (1962); Francis H. Heller, "A Turning Point for Religious Liberty," 29 Va. L. Rev. 440, 452-53 (1943).
[13] Alpheus Thomas Mason, Harlan Fiske Stone: Pillar of the Law 532 (1956).
[14] John T. Noonan, Jr., The Believer and the Powers That Are 251 (1987).
[15] Victor W. Rotnem & F. G. Folsom, Jr., "Recent Restrictions Upon Religious Liberty," 36 Am. Pol. Sci. Rev. 1053, 1062 (1942).
[16] H. N. Hirsch, The Enigma of Felix Frankfurter 152 (1981).
[17] State v. Lefebvre, 20 A.2d 185, 187 (N.H. 1941).
[18] In re Latrecchia, 26 A.2d 881 (N.J. 1942); State v. Smith, 127 P.2d 518, 522 (Kans. 1942); Bolling v. Superior Court for Clallam Country, 133 P.2d 803, 806 (Wash. 1943).
[19] Jones v. Opelika, 316 U.S. 584, 624 (1942).

Robert H. Jackson. Because of the announcements by Black, Douglas, and Murphy and the change in the Court's composition, a three-judge federal court in 1942 determined that *Gobitis* was no longer binding, even though it had yet to be overruled.[20] Opinions by Rutledge while serving on the D.C. Circuit suggested that he would likely join Stone, Black, Douglas, and Murphy in overturning *Gobitis*.[21]

Legislation that Congress passed in 1942, to codify existing rules and customs for the display and use of the American flag, also shook the foundations of *Gobitis*. Language in the bill indicated a preference for avoiding rigidly enforced flag salutes. After stating that in pledging allegiance to the flag a citizen would extend the right hand, palm upward, toward the flag, the statute further provided: "However, civilians will always show full respect to the flag when the pledge is given by merely standing at attention, men removing the headdress."[22] As interpreted by the Justice Department, this statute challenged the merits of *Gobitis* and undercut the requirement for a compulsory flag salute. The department had been informed that Jehovah's Witnesses would have no objection to standing at attention during the flag-salute exercise.[23] In this way they could demonstrate their love of country without violating their religious beliefs. The Justice Department sent out a memo to all U.S. Attorneys, asking them to call to the attention of local authorities the more flexible standard adopted by Congress.[24]

When the flag-salute issue returned to the Supreme Court, this time involving a West Virginia case, a brief by the ACLU noted that Congress had entered the field by passing legislation. Of "great importance," said the brief, "is the fact that Congress did not deem it wise, or see fit, to impose any penalties for failure to salute the flag."[25]

The Supreme Court overruled *Gobitis* in 1943, almost three years to the date after it was announced.[26] Justice Jackson, for a 6 to 3 majority, wrote a strong defense of religious freedom and the Bill of Rights, but credit for the

---

[20] Barnette v. West Virginia State Board of Ed., 47 F.Supp. 251, 253 (S.D. W.Va. 1942) (three-judge court).
[21] Busey v. District of Columbia, 129 F.2d 24, 38 (D.C. Cir. 1942).
[22] 56 Stat. 380, § 7 (1942).
[23] Rotnem & Folsom, "Recent Restrictions Upon Religious Liberty," 36 Am. Pol. Sci. Rev. at 1064.
[24] Manwaring, Render Upon Caesar, at 188-89.
[25] Brief for American Civil Liberties Union, Amicus Curiae, West Virginia State Board of Education v. Barnette; 40 Landmark Briefs and Arguments of the Supreme Court of the United States: Constitutional Law 177-78 (Gerald Gunther & Gerhard Casper, eds) (hereafter "Landmark Briefs").
[26] West Virginia State Board of Education v. Barnette, 319 U.S. 624 (1943).

liberalized decision deserves to be shared with those who refused to accept the Court's 1940 pronouncements on the meaning of the Constitution, minority rights, and religious liberty and rejected the adoption of a compulsory flag salute in state law.

*Chapter 5*

# RELIGIOUS APPAREL IN THE MILITARY

In 1986, the Supreme Court upheld the authority of the Air Force to prohibit an Orthodox Jew from wearing his yarmulke (skullcap) indoors while on duty. A year later Congress countermanded the Court by passing legislation that directed the Air Force to change its regulation to permit a greater exercise of religious liberty by members of the military services. The more generous scope of religious freedom is thus determined here by Congress.

Simcha Goldman, an Orthodox Jew and ordained rabbi, served as a Captain in the U.S. Air Force and was assigned to a mental health clinic where he worked as a clinical psychologist. While in uniform and on duty he wore a yarmulke at all times. Orthodox Jewish religious practice requires a Jewish male to keep his head covered. Over a three-and-a-half-year period, Goldman wore a yarmulke while in uniform without incident.

Matters changed on May 8, 1981, when the Air Force informed him that wearing a yarmulke violated the military dress code, and he could not wear it indoors while in uniform except while working at the regional hospital. His counsel asked the Air Force to permit an exception but was turned down. On June 23, the Air Force ordered Goldman to stop wearing a yarmulke anywhere while in uniform, including at the regional hospital. Because of the dispute over the yarmulke, a previously positive recommendation for Goldman was withdrawn and replaced by a negative one. He was threatened with court-martial if he continued to wear a yarmulke while in uniform.

Why, after three and a half years, did Goldman's wearing of a yarmulke provoke an incident? In April 1981, the month before he was first warned about wearing the yarmulke, he had appeared at a court-martial proceeding to testify on behalf of the defense (and therefore against the Air Force).

Some Justices noted that the action against Goldman appeared to have a retaliatory motive.[1]

After exhausting administrative remedies, Goldman's attorney went to court to enjoin the Secretary of Defense and the Secretary of the Air Force from preventing Goldman from wearing his yarmulke. A district court decided that Goldman was entitled to a preliminary injunction because he was likely to prevail in claiming that the Air Force regulation violated the First Amendment's free exercise clause. The judge noted that the dispute involved a departmental regulation, not a statute passed "by a coequal branch of government."[2] The district court, therefore, was not colliding with congressional policy. The judge appeared to make light of the Pentagon's position that allowing Goldman to wear his yarmulke "will crush the spirit of uniformity, which in turn will weaken the will and fighting ability of the Air Force."[3]

Another lawsuit from the same circuit involved a different Orthodox Jew who also challenged the Air Force policy on yarmulkes. In this case a district judge sided with the Air Force, concluding that departures from uniformity would adversely affect "the promotion of teamwork, counteract pride and motivation, and undermine discipline and morale, all to the detriment of the substantial compelling governmental interest of maintaining an efficient Air Force."[4]

These two conflicting decisions reached the D.C. Circuit. Almost three years elapsed before it issued a ruling on the Goldman case. All three judges on the panel agreed that the Air Force was justified in adopting and enforcing its regulation, notwithstanding Goldman's First Amendment rights.[5] The Air Force argued that if it accommodated Goldman on his yarmulke, other military personnel would offer religious reasons to use turbans, robes, face and body paint, shorn hair, unshorn hair, badges, rings, amulets, bracelets, jodhpurs, and symbolic daggers.[6] The D.C. Circuit voted against a motion to rehear the case en banc.[7]

Rulings by the D.C. Circuit triggered legislative activity by Congress. As an amendment to the defense authorization bill in 1984, Representative Stephen Solarz proposed that members of the armed forces may wear

---

[1] Goldman v. Weinberger, 475 U.S. 503, 511 (1986) (concurrence by Justice Stevens, joined by Justices White and Powell).
[2] Goldman v. Secretary of Defense, 530 F.Supp. 12, 15 (D.D.C. 1981).
[3] Id. at 16.
[4] Bitterman v. Secretary of Defense, 553 F.Supp. 719, 725 (D.D.C. 1982).
[5] Goldman v. Secretary of Defense, 734 F.2d 1531, 1535 (D.C. Cir. 1984).
[6] Id. at 1539.
[7] Goldman v. Secretary of Defense, 739 F.2d 657 (D.C. Cir. 1984).

unobtrusive religious headgear, such as a skullcap, if religious observances or practices require the wearing of such headgear. Under this amendment, offered for a one-year trial period, the Defense Department could prohibit the headgear if it interfered with the performance of military duties.[8] His amendment was accepted.[9] However, the conferees decided to eliminate the Solarz language and replace it with a requirement that the Defense Department report on changes in service regulations that would promote the free expression of religion to the greatest extent possible consistent with the requirements of military discipline.[10] This lengthy study, touching on a broad range of issues, concluded that courts would most likely defer to the military services regarding the wearing of yarmulkes.[11]

The Supreme Court accepted Goldman's case for review. During oral argument, Kathryn Oberly of the Justice Department advised the Court to stay out of the battle and leave the dispute to the elected branches: "If Congress thinks that further accom[m]odation is either required or desirable it can legislate it."[12] In the event that Congress made a mistake it would be relatively easy to correct it with new legislation, but if the Court tried to constitutionalize mandatory exceptions to the uniform requirements, it would be "far more difficult for what might turn out to be a mistake in judgment about the effect on discipline and morale to be corrected."[13]

The Court, divided 5 to 4, held that the First Amendment did not prohibit the Air Force regulation, even though Goldman's religious belief required the wearing of a yarmulke. The Court accepted the judgment of the Air Force that the outfitting of military personnel in standardized uniforms "encourages the subordination of personal preferences and identities in favor of the overall group mission."[14] For the Court, the values of uniformity, hierarchy, unity, discipline and obedience justified the regulation.

In a dissent, Justice Brennan (joined by Justice Marshall) presented conflicting views on which branch of government is responsible for protecting individual rights. First he claimed that the Court's decision represented an abdication of its role "as principal expositor of the Constitution and protector of individual liberties in favor of credulous deference to unsupported assertions of military necessity."[15] Yet later he

---

[8] 130 Cong. Rec. 14295 (1984).
[9] Id. at 14298.
[10] H. Rept. No. 98-1080, 98th Cong., 2d Sess. 293-94 (1984); 98 Stat. 2532-33, § 554 (1984).
[11] Joint Service Study on Religious Matters 21, 25 (March 1985).
[12] Oral argument, Goldman v. Weinberger, U.S. Supreme Court, January 14, 1986, at 45.
[13] Id.
[14] Goldman v. Weinberger, 475 U.S. 503, 508 (1986).
[15] Id. at 514.

acknowledged that other parts of government also protect religious freedom: "Guardianship of this precious liberty is not the exclusive domain of federal courts. It is the responsibility as well of the States and of the other branches of the Federal Government."[16] His concluding sentence pointed toward the remedy: "The Court and the military have refused these servicemen their constitutional rights; we must hope that Congress will correct this wrong."[17]

Congress had unquestioned constitutional authority to tell the Air Force to change the regulation. The Constitution provides that Congress shall "make rules for the Government and Regulation of the land and naval forces."[18] Within two weeks of the Court's decision, legislation was introduced to permit members of the armed forces to wear items of apparel not part of the official uniform. Members of the military could wear any "neat, conservative, and unobtrusive" item of apparel to satisfy the tenets of a religious belief. The Secretary of the military service would have authority to prohibit the wearing of the item after determining that it "significantly interferes with the performance of the member's military duties."[19]

In the defense authorization bill in 1986, the House Armed Services Committee included a provision regarding the wearing of neat and conservative religious apparel by members of the armed forces while in uniform. The phrase "neat and conservative" was lifted from military service regulations. In acknowledging the importance of uniformity, cohesion, and esprit, the committee denied that the wearing of yarmulkes or turbans "would necessarily threaten good order, discipline, or morale in the armed forces."[20]

The provision remained in the bill as passed by the House, but lost narrowly in the Senate. An amendment to permit members of the military to wear, under certain circumstances, religious apparel not part of the official uniform, was tabled by a vote of 51 to 49.[21] Senator Barry Goldwater, chairman of the Senate Armed Services Committee, strongly opposed the amendment, warning that Muslims would insist on wearing the dress and gear of a Muslim, Hopi Indians would wear a red band around their head and

---

[16] Id. at 523.
[17] Id. at 524.
[18] U.S. Const., art. I, § 8, cl. 14.
[19] 132 Cong. Rec. 6655 (1986) (Senator Alfonse D'Amato); id. at 7042, 7211 (Senator Frank Lautenberg).
[20] H. Rept. No. 99-718, 99th Cong. 2d Sess. 200, 488 (1986). See also 132 Cong. Rec. 20644 (1986).
[21] 132 Cong. Rec. 19808 (1986).

other Indians would want to wear feather headdresses.[22] When the bill reached conference, the House provision was dropped.[23]

The following year, the House again added language to permit the wearing of neat and conservative religious apparel by the military while in uniform, provided it did not interfere with the performance of military duties. No one spoke against the amendment. Senate debate was more spirited, but this time the provision passed 55 to 42. The Senate's reversal reflected some switches by Senators and the results of the 1986 elections. Six Senators (Boschwitz, Burdick, Danforth, Domenici, Harkin, and Rockefeller) switched from favoring the 1986 tabling motion to favoring the 1987 amendment. Eight new Senators (Adams, Breaux, Daschle, Graham, Karnes, Milkulski, Reid, and Wirth) voted for the 1987 amendment. Other adjustments brought the final tally to 55.[24]

The statutory language allows members of the armed services to wear an item of religious apparel while in uniform. The Secretary of a service may prohibit the wearing of an item of religious appeal when the Secretary determines that it would interfere with the performance of the member's military duties, or if the Secretary determines that the item is not neat and conservative. The statute applies only to the wearing of religious apparel that is part of the observance of religious faith practiced by the member.[25]

---

[22] Id. at 19802.
[23] H. Rept. No. 1001, 99th cong., 2d sess. 474 (1986).
[24] Senators Gore and Simon, who opposed the 1986 tabling motion, did not vote on the 1987 amendment. Senators Byrd, Nickles, and Johnston switched from opposing the 1986 tabling motion to opposing the 1987 amendment. Three Senators (Mathias, Hart, and Hawkins) who opposed the 1986 tabling motion did not return in 1987.
[25] 101 Stat. 1086-87, § 508 (1987).

*Chapter 6*

# SCHOOL PRAYER

Sometimes Congress protects religious liberty by going against Court rulings. On other occasions it protects religious liberty by supporting the Court. It performed the latter role in the controversial case of *Engel* v. *Vitale* (1962), which struck down New York's "Regents' Prayer" that required children in public schools to say a prayer directed by the teacher. Although some Members of Congress responded with constitutional amendments to overturn *Engel* and with legislation to remove the Court's jurisdiction to hear such cases, these court-curbing efforts were repeatedly rejected. Even constitutional amendments that supposedly overturned the 1962 decision in fact respected its key holding.

The Court held that the New York prayer was unconstitutional because "it is no part of the business of government to compose official prayers for any group of the American people to recite as a part of a religious program carried on by government."[1] The Court did not rule against prayer. It ruled against the government's involvement in drafting a prayer to be said by students compelled to attend school.

The New York program, as modified and approved by state courts, did not require all students to recite the prayer. It permitted students "who wish to do so to remain silent or be excused from the room."[2] This procedure appeared to make the prayer discretionary, not compulsory. However, Justice Black, writing for the Court, noted that when the "power, prestige and

---

[1] Engel v. Vitale, 370 U.S. 421, 425 (1962). New York law directed that the following prayer be said aloud by each class of a public school at the beginning of the day: "Almighty God, we acknowledge our dependence upon Thee, and we beg Thy blessings upon us, our parents, our teachers, and our Country."

[2] Id. at 430.

financial support of government is placed behind a particular religious belief, the indirect coercive pressure upon religious minorities to conform to the prevailing officially approved religion is plain."[3] It would be difficult for a child to remain silent or ask to be excused from the room.

Some Members of Congress accused the Court of being hostile to religion. Senator Sam J. Ervin, Jr. announced that the Court "has held that God is unconstitutional." Representative Mendel Rivers criticized "this bold, malicious, atheistic and sacrilegious twist of this unpredictable group of uncontrolled despots." Representative William Arthur Winstead wondered whether the Court "is trying to drive God and religion out of our schools and even out of our heritage."[4]

If one follows the development of the case, however, there was no intent on the part of the Court or the litigants to be hostile to religion or to prayer. During oral argument, the attorney for the plaintiffs opposing the Regents' Prayer strongly endorsed religion and prayer. He told the Justices: "I come here not as an antagonist of religion; ... my clients are deeply religious people; ... I say prayer is good. My clients say prayer is good."[5] In writing for the majority, Justice Black tried to steer clear of any animosity toward religion:

> It has been argued that to apply the Constitution in such a way as to prohibit state laws respecting an establishment of religious services in public schools is to indicate a hostility toward religion or toward prayer. Nothing, of course, could be more wrong. The history of man is inseparable from the history of religion.... It is neither sacrilegious nor antireligious to say that each separate government in this country should stay out of the business of writing or sanctioning official prayers and leave that purely religious function to the people themselves and to those the people choose to look to for religious guidance.[6]

This intent by Justice Black was undercut by a concurrence written by Justice Douglas and by statements issued by some members of the public. Douglas suggested that the decision might prohibit other ceremonial observations of a religious nature, such as the Court's traditional invocation when it convenes and the offering of a daily prayer by a chaplain in Congress. Those conjectures, totally unrelated to the issue before the Court, helped fuel public confusion and outrage. Justice Stewart's dissent also

---

[3] Id. at 431.
[4] 108 Cong. Rec. 11709, 11732, 12227 (1962).
[5] 56 Landmark Briefs 1038.
[6] 370 U.S. at 433-35.

strayed far afield. He did not want to deny school children their "wish" to recite the prayer or to interfere with those "who want to begin their day by joining in prayer." The case before the Court had nothing to do with the desire of children to pray on their own initiative. The issue was solely the constitutionality of a state composing an official prayer for minors in public schools. After reading the decision, constitutional law scholar Philip Kurland had the impression of the majority "walking on eggs and of the two minority Justices stamping after them."[7]

Douglas's concurrence became the focal point of congressional hearings, held shortly after the decision was issued. "Again and again witnesses pointed to it as an example of what the Court would do in the future."[8] More striking, the prayer was greatly misrepresented by the President of the American Bar Association, who claimed that the decision would require elimination of the motto "In God We Trust" from all coins.[9] That issue was never before the Court, either expressly or by implication. The public impression never recovered from these misleading readings.

The day following *Engel*, Representative Frank Becker introduced this constitutional amendment: "Prayers may be offered in the course of any program in any public school or other public place in the United States."[10] That language did not directly challenge the Court's decision, which was restricted to the government's role in *composing* prayer and using coercion. Becker's language a year later, drafted with other members, was even more in line with *Engel*: "Nothing in this Constitution shall be deemed to prohibit the offering, reading from or listening to prayers or biblical scriptures, if participation therein is on a voluntary basis, in any governmental or public school, institution, or place."[11] *Engel* focused not on voluntary prayer but state-ordered prayer.

Despite all the criticism directed at *Engel*, none of the versions of constitutional amendments offered by Members of Congress and Presidents attempted to overturn the Court's holding. One month after the Court's decision, the Senate Judiciary Committee held two days of hearings to explore the issue of prayers in public schools. The hearings allowed critics to lambast the Court, but no steps were taken to reverse the Court. The

---

[7] Philip B. Kurland, "The Regents' Prayer Case: 'Full of Sound and Fury, Signifying...,'" 1962 Sup. Ct. Rev. 1, 13 (1962).

[8] William M. Beaney & Edward N. Beiser, "Prayer and Politics: The Impact of Engel and Schempp on the Political Process," 13 J. Pub. L. 475, 479 (1964).

[9] Chester A. Newland, "Press Coverage of the United States Supreme Court," 17 West. Pol. Q. 15, 28 (1964).

[10] H. J. Res. 752, 87th Cong., 2d Sess. (1962).

[11] 109 Cong. Rec. 16700 (1963).

committee did not issue a final report, nor did it propose remedial legislation.[12]

When the House Judiciary Committee finally held hearings in 1964 on a constitutional amendment to reverse the Court, most of the religious organizations testified in favor of *Engel*. They understood that their united opposition to the amendment would make it "respectable" and "safe" for legislators to vote against the Becker proposal. With one religious leader after another testifying against the amendment, Becker and his supporters were in no position to argue that only the godless opposed them.[13] Protestant and Jewish groups generally found fault with the amendment; Catholic leaders were divided.[14]

In 1966, Senator Everett Dirksen offered a constitutional amendment to permit "the voluntary participation by students or others in prayer. Nothing contained in this article shall authorize any such [school] authority to prescribe the form or content of any prayer."[15] Obviously the amendment was drafted with great care to avoid a collision with *Engel*. His amendment attracted a vote of 49 to 37, or nine votes short of the necessary two-thirds.[16]

Over the next three decades, several hundred constitutional amendments were introduced to permit school prayer. Not one succeeded.[17] Even when opponents of the Court drafted these amendments, they never disturbed *Engel's* fundamental principle that government officials should not compose school prayers for public school students to recite. For example, the Republican Platform of 1964 offered constitutional language to permit individuals and groups "who choose to do so to exercise their religion freely in public places, provided religious exercises are not *prepared or prescribed* by the state or political subdivision thereof and no person's participation therein is coerced, thus preserving the traditional separation of church and state."[18]

---

[12] "Prayers in Public Schools and Other Matters," hearings before the Senate Committee on the Judiciary, 87th Cong., 2d Sess. (1962); William M. Beaney & Edward N. Beiser, "Prayer and Politics: The Impact of Engel and Schempp on the Political Process," 13 J. Pub. L. 475, 480 (1964).

[13] Beaney & Beiser, "Prayer and Politics," 13 J. Pub. L. at 497, 499-500.

[14] 1964 CQ Almanac 399; "School Prayers," hearings before the House Committee on the Judiciary, 88th Cong., 2d Sess. (1964). For excerpts from these hearings, see Louis Fisher, American Constitutional Law 681-82 (4th ed. 2001).

[15] 112 Cong. Rec. 23555 (1966).

[16] Id. at 23556.

[17] John R. Vile, Encyclopedia of Constitutional Amendments, Proposed Amendments, and Amending Issues 237-39 (1996).

[18] 2 Donald Bruce Johnson, National Party Platforms, 1960-1976, at 683 (1978) (emphasis added).

Although President Ronald Reagan stated that the Court had "ruled wrongly" on school prayer,[19] and announced in his 1983 State of the Union Message that "God should never have been expelled from America's classrooms,"[20] none of the constitutional amendments proposed during his Administration directly challenged *Engel*.[21] For example, in 1982 Reagan proposed this amendment: "Nothing in this Constitution shall be construed to prohibit individual or group prayer in public schools or other public institutions. No person shall be required by the United States or by any State to participate in prayer."[22] When this amendment was reported by the Senate Judiciary Committee in 1984, it included this last sentence: "Neither the United States nor any state shall compose the words of any prayer to be said in public schools."[23] The committee amendment was accepted 96 to zero, but the amendment as a whole received a vote of only 56-44, or eleven votes short of the required two thirds.[24]

In 1998, when the House voted on a constitutional amendment to permit school prayer, the language provided that "Government shall not require any person to join in prayer or other religious activity, [or] initiate or designate school prayers."[25] The amendment failed on a vote of 224 to 203, or 61 votes short.[26] Constitutional amendments and statutory proposals are now likely to focus on voluntary prayer or a "moment of silence."[27]

In addition to constitutional amendments, there have been several efforts by Members of Congress to strip the federal courts of jurisdiction to hear school prayer cases. Under Article III of the Constitution, the Supreme Court is given appellate jurisdiction "with such exceptions, and under such Regulations as the Congress shall make." The court-stripping initiatives offered in response to *Engel* were nevertheless aimed at *voluntary* prayer. Offered from 1962 to 1988, they have all failed.[28]

Some of the criticism of *Engel* has eased as a result of religious groups gaining "equal access" to school buildings. This movement reflects the efforts of both the Supreme Court and Congress. In 1981, the Supreme Court held that state universities could not allow student secular groups to meet in university buildings but deny the same privilege to student religious

---

[19] Public Papers of the Presidents, 1981, at 958.
[20] Public Papers of the Presidents, 1983, I, at 106-07.
[21] See Fisher, Religious Liberty in America, at 132-34.
[22] Public Papers of the Presidents, 1982, I, 647-48.
[23] 130 Cong. Rec. 4318 (1984).
[24] Id. at 5421, 5919.
[25] 144 Cong. Rec. H4078 (daily ed. June 4, 1998).
[26] Id. at H4112.
[27] Fisher, Religious Liberty in America, at 139-40, 142-46.
[28] Id. at 129-32.

groups.[29] Congress extended this same right to public secondary schools. Congressional hearings in 1983 focused on legislation that would require student religious groups to be afforded the same rights as other student groups to meet on student grounds in secondary schools.[30] Religious groups and civil rights organizations were divided on the merits of the bill.[31]

The Equal Access Act of 1984 states that it shall be unlawful for any public secondary schools that receives federal funds "to deny equal access or a fair opportunity to, or discriminate against, any student who wish to conduct a meeting within that limited open forum on the basis of religious, political, philosophical, or other content of the speech at such meetings.[32] The Supreme Court upheld this statute.[33] Decisions in 1993 and 2001 widened student access to after-hour religious activities.[34]

---

[29] Widmar v. Vincent, 454 U.S. 263 (1981).

[30] "Equal Access: A First Amendment Question," hearings before the Senate Committee on the Judiciary, 98th Cong. 1st Sess. (1983); "Hearings on the Equal Access Act," hearings before the House Committee on Education and Labor, 98th Cong., 1st Sess. (1983).

[31] Fisher, Religious Liberty in America, at 135.

[32] 98 Stat. 1302-04 (1984).

[33] Westside Community Bd. of Ed. v. Mergens, 496 U.S. 226 (1990). Two years after the Equal Access Act, the Court vacated a Third Circuit decision for lack of standing to appeal. The case involved the right of high school students to form religious groups and meet in schoolrooms. Bender v. Williamsport Area School Dist., 475 U.S. 534 (1986).

[34] In 1993, the Court ruled that if states permit school property to be used after hours for social, civil, and recreational purposes, they may not discriminate on the basis of religious viewpoint. Lamb's Chapel v. Center Moriches School Dist., 508 U.S. 384 (1993). The decision in 2001 applied to elementary schools the same principle of equal access that had been applied to public rush schools and universities. Good News Club v. Milford Central School, 533 U.S. 98 (2001).

Because of these congressional and judicial actions, students now have much greater opportunity to pray and study religion in public schools. In 1995, in a memorandum to the Secretary of Education and the Attorney General, President Bill Clinton set forth the principles for religious expression in public schools. Students have the right to engage in individual or group prayer and religious discussing during the school day. They may read their Bibles or other scripture, say grace before meals, and pray and discuss their religious views in informal settings, such as cafeterias and hallways. They may participate in events, before and after school, with religious content. School officials may neither discourage nor encourage these activities.[35] Studies indicate that students in public schools are active in prayer clubs and other religious activities.[36]

---

[35] Public Papers of the Presidents, 1995, II, at 1083-85.
[36] Fisher, Religious Liberty in America, at 141.

*Chapter 7*

# AMERICAN INDIAN RELIGIOUS FREEDOM

For most of U.S. history, little was done at the national or state level to protect the religious practices of American Indians. There were few efforts by governmental institutions or private societies to safeguard and preserve the unique religious beliefs of Indian tribes. Only in recent decades has the national government taken steps to secure the religious heritage of Indians, and that initiative has come largely from the political branches. An expansion of Indian religious rights has depended primarily on statutes, presidential leadership, agency regulations, and the political process.

To the extent that government considered religion in the lives of Indians, it was to provide funds and assistance to convert Indians to Christianity.[1] Non-Indian religious missions demonstrated little interest or respect for Indian religious beliefs. For the most part, they attacked Indian religions and relegated Indian religious beliefs nd ritual practices "to the realm of superstition."[2]

Toward the end of the nineteenth century, a number of Indian religious practices were curbed. Many Indian children were taken from their families and placed in boarding schools for up to eight years, where they learned English, wore Western-style clothing, and had their hair cut Western-style. Anything Indian, including dress, language, and religious practice, was

---

[1] Id. at 147-51.
[2] R. Pierce Beaver, "Protestant Churches and the Indians," in 4 Handbook of North American Indians 439 (William C. Sturtevant ed 1988). See also Robert F. Berkhofer, Jr., Salvation and the Savage: An Analysis of Protestant Missions and American Indian Response, 1787-1862 (1965).

eliminated to the greatest extent possible.[3] Administrative officials declared Indian funeral ceremonies illegal and banned the Sun Dance (requiring the individual to thrust a sharpened stick through his skin) in 1881. Some government officials and Army officers thought that every Indian dance was a war dance. Misapprehension about the "ghost dance," which promised Indians that they could meet their dead relatives, led to tragedy. With Indians wearing ghost shirts painted with magic symbols and moving in a hypnotic state, whites feared a major Indian uprising. Later, the massacre at Wounded Knee in 1890 killed two hundred or more Indians and twenty-nine whites.[4]

Circulars issued by the Office of Indian Affairs from 1921 to 1923 expressed satisfaction that Indian dances were growing less frequent and had fewer "barbaric features," but noted that on a number of reservations, "the native dance still has enough evil tendencies to furnish a retarding influence." The Sun Dance and similar dances were considered "Indian Offenses" under departmental regulations, with "corrective penalties" provided. One of the circulars offered a number of recommendations, including that "none take part in the dances or be present who are under 50 years of age."[5] Dances of supposed sexual excess, such as the Hopi Snake Dance, were singled out for criticism.

One of the reformers who fought to safeguard Indian religious beliefs and practices was John Collier, Executive Secretary of the American Indian Defense Association. In 1923 he testified at House hearings in defense of Indian dances. When a Member of Congress drafted legislation in 1926 to empower Indian superintendents to jail reservation Indians for six months without trial or review, under regulations drawn up by the Interior Department, Collier successfully fought against the bill and prevented it from being reported out of committee.[6]

In 1928, the Institute for Government Research published a comprehensive work entitled *The Problem of Indian Administration.* Referred to as "The Meriam Report" because of its technical director, Lewis Meriam, the study was highly critical of U.S. policy toward the Indians. It noted the "common failure to study sympathetically and understandingly the Indians' own religions and ethics and to use what is good in them as the

---

[3] Peter Farb, Man's Rise to Civilization as Shown by the Indian of North America from Primeval Times to the Coming of the Industrial State 257 (1968).
[4] David E. Witheridge, "No Freedom of Religion for American Indians," 18 J. Church & State 5, 14-15 (1976); Dee Brown, Bury My Heart at Wounded Knee (1971).
[5] "The Denial of Indian Civil and Religious Rights," 8 Indian Historian 43, 44 (1975); see also Francis Paul Prucha, The Great Father 800-06 (1995).
[6] Kenneth Philp, "John Collier and the Crusade to Protect Indian Religious Freedom, 1920-26," 1 J. Ethnic Studies 22, 33-34 (1973).

foundation upon which to build.... The attempt blindly to destroy the whole Indian religion may in effect be an attack on some of the very elements of religious belief which the missionary himself espouses and which he hopes the Indian will adopt."[7]

Collier became Commissioner of Indian Affairs in 1934 and remained in that position under 1945. He helped persuade Congress to repeal a number of obsolete laws that covered Indians, some of which had prohibited the sending or carrying of seditious messages and any correspondence with foreign nations to excite Indians to war. The repeal statute passed in 1934 without debate.[8] In that same year, Collier issued an order expressing the policy of the Indian Office regarding religion:

> No interference with Indian religious life or ceremonial expression will hereafter be tolerated.... Violations of law or of the proprieties, if committed under the cloak of any religion, Indian or other, or any cultural tradition, Indian or other, are to be dealt with as such, but in no case shall punishment for statutory violations or for improprieties be so administered as to constitute an interference with, or to imply censorship over, the religious or cultural life, Indian or other.
>
> The fullest constitutional liberty, in all matters affecting religion, conscience and culture, is insisted on for all Indians.[9]

Federal policy in Indian affairs changed in the late 1940s and 1950s. Proposals were offered to "emancipate" Indians from the Bureau of Indian Affairs (BIA), eliminate BIA services, and transfer the BIA from the Interior Department to a new department — the Federal Security Agency — with the goal of integrating Indians into the general population. Included in these reforms was the termination of all federal supervision and control over Indians and the transfer of federal responsibilities to the states. This termination policy was criticized by Presidents John F. Kennedy, Lyndon B. Johnson, and Richard Nixon.[10]

Beginning in 1962, Congress passed a number of bills to protect Indian religious freedom, covering such areas as eagle feathers, Indian civil rights, Taos religious shrines, an Indian religious freedom statute, the Klamath Indians, and the protection of Indian graves and funereal objects.

---

[7] The Problem of Indian Administration 845-46 (1928).
[8] 48 Stat. 787 (1934); S. Rept. No. 634, 73d Cong., 2d Sess. (1934); 78 Cong. Rec. 7271, 8222, 8351, 8361, 8447-48, 8607 (1934).
[9] 2 Stokes 452. See Kenneth R. Philp, John Collier's Crusade for Indian Reform, 1920-1954 (1977).
[10] Fisher, Religious Liberty in America, at 160-62.

## EAGLE FEATHERS

One of the first Indian religious issues addressed by Congress concerned legislation to protect eagles. Legislation adopted in 1940 protected the bald eagle, and in 1962 Congress returned to this subject by enacting legislation to protect golden eagles.[11] The legislative history of this second statute explains the importance of the eagle for many Indian tribes, particularly in the Southwest, that performed ceremonies of religious significance. The legislation authorized the Secretary of the Interior to issue regulations allowing exceptions for various reasons, including "the religious purposes of Indian tribes."

In defining the possession and use of eagles for religious purposes, a regulation issued in 1963 restricted permits to Indians "who are authentic, bona fide practitioners of such religion."[12] Current regulations require an applicant to be "an Indian who is authorized to participate in *bona fide* tribal religious ceremonies."[13] Litigation has clarified some issues that have developed on the application of the Bald Eagle Protection Act to Indian religious practices.[14] On April 29, 1994, President Clinton issued a memorandum concerning the distribution of eagle feathers for Indian religious purposes. He said that eagle feathers "hold a sacred place in Native American culture and religious practices," and that the Administration had changed its policy and procedures to "facilitate the collection and distribution of scarce eagle bodies and parts for this purpose." He directed executive departments and agencies to work cooperatively with tribal governments to accommodate Native American religious practices "to the fullest extent under the law."[15]

---

[11] 54 Stat. 250 (1940); 76 Stat. 1246 (1962).
[12] 28 Fed. Reg. 976, § 11.5 (1963).
[13] 50 C.F.R. § 22.22 (c)(2) (10-1-01 ed.) (emphasis in original).
[14] United States v. Dion, 476 U.S. 734 (1986), rev'g United States v. Dion, 752 F.2d 1261 (8th Cir. 1985); Andrus v. Allard, 444 U.S. 51 (1979); United States v. Abeyta, 632 F.Supp. 1301 (D. N.M. 1986); United States v. Dion, 762 F.2d 674 (8th Cir. 1985); United States v. Fryberg, 622 F.2d 1010 (9th Cir. 1980); United States v. Top Sky, 547 F.2d 486 (9th Cir. 1976); United States v. White, 508 F.2d 454 (8th Cir. 1974). See John Geb, "Native American Culture: The Use of Feathers as a Protected Right," 2 Am. Ind. L. Rev. 105 (1974).
[15] 59 Fed. Reg. 22953 (1994).

## THE INDIAN CIVIL RIGHTS ACT

In 1968, as part of an omnibus bill providing penalties for certain acts of violence or intimidation, Congress passed what is called the Indian Civil Rights Act. Actually, it reads more like a bill of rights, covering First Amendment rights, protections against unreasonable searches and seizures, safeguards of criminal proceedings, denial of equal protection, and deprivation of liberty or property without due process of law.

Federal courts had decided that in cases of religious liberty, neither the First Amendment nor the Fourteenth Amendment applied to Indian tribal governments, and that Congress had not passed legislation making those constitutional provisions applicable to Indian nations.[16] Senator Sam Ervin (D-N.C.) took the lead in extending constitutional rights to Indians.[17] The statute offers protections to individuals and imposes restrictions on government, in this case the tribal governments. Thus, no Indian tribe exercising powers of self-government shall "make or enforce any law prohibiting the free exercise of religion."[18] Because some tribes have a theocratic foundation, an establishment of religion clause was not included. An Establishment Clause might have worked "to the disadvantage of tribal religion."[19]

## TAOS RELIGIOUS SHRINES

In 1969, the House Committee on Interior and Insular Affairs reported legislation to grant to the Pueblo de Taos Indians in New Mexico trust title to approximately 48,000 acres of federally owned land that had been taken from the Indians in 1906, by presidential order, without payment of any compensation. Congress had passed legislation in 1933 to give the Pueblo a 50-year special use permit to the area,[20] but the Taos Indians wanted a more permanent arrangement. Placing great significance on the land, they urged the government to return the title to the land rather than compensate them with money. The Indians argued that preservation of the area and placing limits on non-Indian use were essential in protecting religious interests and

---

[16] Native American Church v. Navajo Tribal Council, 272 F.2d 131 (10th Cir. 1959).
[17] Prucha, The Great Father, at 1106-07.
[18] 82 Stat. 77, § 202(1) (1968).
[19] Milner S. Ball, "Constitution, Court, Indian Tribes," 1987 Am. Bar Foundation Research J. 1, 132 (1987).
[20] 48 Stat. 109, § 4 (1933).

the sacredness of the land. The integrity of their religion, they said, required complete privacy.[21] The most sacred shrine hi the area is the Blue Lake.

On the choice between payment and conveying land, the House Committee on Interior and Insular Affairs concluded that "the equities are on the side of the Indians" and that land should be restored to the Pueblo.[22] The bill passed the House in 1969 by voice vote, with little opposition.[23] During Senate debate, Senator George McGovern explained that the bill protected "a deeply spiritual and religious matter, which goes right to the heart of freedom of religion and freedom of conscience in our country, because the Blue Lake area which is in dispute, and which has been in dispute for so many years, is regarded as the most sacred of all places by the Indian people, and particularly the Taos Pueblo Indians."[24] After two days of debate, the Senate passed the bill by a vote of 70 to 12, and it became law. The statute refers to the land "as the scene of certain religious ceremonials."[25]

## AMERICAN INDIAN RELIGIOUS FREEDOM ACT

In 1978, Congress passed a joint resolution expressing the principles of religious freedom for Indians. The resolution, called the American Indian Religious Freedom Act (AIRFA), begins by recognizing that freedom of religion is an "inherent right" for all people and "fundamental to the democratic structure of the United States." Moreover, the individual right to practice religion has produced "a rich variety of religious heritages in this country." Included within this culture are the religious practices of the American Indian, "such practices forming the basis of Indian identity and value systems." After citing the instances in which federal laws and practices had abridged and infringed on the religious freedom of American Indians, the legislation resolves that "henceforth it shall be the policy of the United States to protect and preserve for American Indians their inherent right of freedom to believe, express, and exercise the traditional religions of the American Indian, Eskimo, Aleut, and Native Hawaiians, including but not limited to access to sites, use and possession of sacred objects, and the freedom to worship through ceremonials and traditional rites."[26]

---

[21] H. Rept. No. 91-326, 91st Cong., 1st Sess. 2 (1969).
[22] Id. at 3.
[23] 115 Cong. Rec. 24871, 24878-86 (1969).
[24] 116 Cong. Rec. 39331 (1970).
[25] 84 Stat. 1437 (1970). See S. Rept. No. 91-345, 91st Cong., 2d Sess. (1970); 116 Cong. Rec. 39327-38, 39586-610 (1970).
[26] 92 Stat. 469 (1978).

The resolution expressed only a general policy and lacked enforcement mechanisms. As the floor manager in the House said: "It has no teeth in it."[27] Still, it demonstrates an awareness of and a sensitivity to Indian religious freedom that was not likely to have been expressed by Congress (or any other branch of government) in previous years. Moreover, it formed a foundation for subsequent legislative acts that protected Indian religious liberty.

In litigation that refers to AIRFA, courts balance the government's interest in assuring public access to natural attractions with the Indians' free exercise of religion. In such balancing tests, courts typically uphold public access.[28] With such outcomes in the courts, the burden is placed on Congress to legislate specific protections for Indian religious liberty, and it has done that several times.

This type of judicial appeal to Congress appeared in a 1988 decision by the Supreme Court. It held that the federal government had not violated the Free Exercise Clause by permitting timber harvesting and construction of a road through a portion of a national forest that has traditionally been used for Indian religious purposes.[29] Writing for the majority, Justice O'Connor emphasized that remedies would have to be found outside the Court. She noted that the Constitution "does not, and courts cannot, offer to reconcile the various competing demands on government, many of them rooted in sincere religious belief, that inevitably arise in so diverse a society as ours. That task, to the extent that it is feasible, is for the legislature and other institutions."[30] An example of Congress accepting that responsibility is discussed next.

## KLAMATH INDIANS

Twice in the 1980s, Congress passed legislation to recognize the rights of Klamath Indians in Oregon. In 1980, a private law set aside in special trust status certain lands in the Winema National Forest for a member of the Klamath Indian nation, Edison Chiloquin. As part of the "termination" policy in the 1950s, federal supervision over Klamath Indian property came

---

[27] 124 Cong. Rec. 21445 (Rep. Morris Udall).
[28] Wilson v. Block, 708 F.2d 735 (D.C. Cir. 1983); Crow v. Gullet, 706 F.2d 856 (8th Or. 1983); Badoni v. Higginson, 638 F.2d 172 (10th Cir. 1980), cert, denied, 452 U.S. 954 (1981); Sequoyah v. Tennessee Valley Authority, 620 F.2d 1159 (6th Cir. 1980), cert, denied, 449 U.S. 953 (1980).
[29] Lyng v. Northwest Indian Cemetery Prot. Assn., 485 U.S. 439 (1988).
[30] Id. at 452.

to an end. Adult members of the tribe were given the option of holding their interests in common under Oregon law or converting the interests to cash. In a 1958 election, approximately 77 percent of the tribal members voted to sell their property. Edison Chiloquin and others wanted to retain their interests in the land. As a result of the election, 631,000 acres were sold to a private corporation (91,000 acres), the Department of Interior (15,000 acres), and the Department of Agriculture (525,000).[31] The government used the land to create the Winema National Forest.

In 1969, a majority of the remaining holders of trust elected to terminate the trust. Legislation in 1973 directed the Secretary of Agriculture to acquire 135,000 acres of land to be added to the Winema National Forest. Purchase of the land resulted in the disbursement of $270,000 to each Indian beneficiary. Chiloquin, who had helped create the "Committee to Save the Remaining Klamath Indian Lands," refused to accept the money. Instead, he wanted land to establish a village founded on traditional values and the preservation of Indian culture, ways, and spiritual beliefs. To underscore his determination, he built a tipi in the forest, became a squatter, and kept a sacred council fire lit.

A private bill was introduced in Congress to support Chiloquin's objectives. The purpose of the bill, as Senator Mark Hatfield said, was to avoid "confrontation and all other kinds of unpleasantries of trying to expel this man from the lands that are his ancestral home."[32] The bill specified that the land set aside for Chiloquin "shall not be inconsistent with its cultural, historical, and archeological character." If the land were used by Chiloquin or his heirs for other than "traditional Indian purposes," it would revert to the United States to protect archeological, cultural, and traditional values associated with the property."[33]

A second statute gave assistance to the Klamaths. Although they had long been recognized by the federal government as an Indian tribe, in 1954, as part of the termination policy, Congress passed legislation terminating federal supervision over the tribe and putting an end to federal services for tribal members. As already explained, the termination statute gave members a choice of either withdrawing from the tribe and taking their share of the

---

[31] Background on the Edison Chiloquin bill comes from H. Rept. No. 1406, 96th Cong., 2d Sess. (1980) and Garrett Epps, To an Unknown God: Religious Freedom on Trial 49-52 (2001). See also Theodore Stern, The Klamath Tribe: A People and Their Reservation 249- 52 (1965).

[32] 126 Cong. Rec. 30379 (1980).

[33] 94 Stat. 3613 (1980).

sale of land in cash, or remaining with the tribe and keeping their share in trust.[34]

In reporting remedial legislation in 1986, the House Committee on Interior and Insular Affairs said that the government had never properly asked tribal members whether they were in favor of the 1954 bill. In fact, the tribe had voted to send a slate of delegates to Congress to state their opposition to the bill.[35] Legislation in 1986 restored federal recognition to the Klamath Indian tribes. Rights and privileges that may have been lost because of the 1954 statute were once again protected. Any federal services and benefits given to Indian tribes recognized by the federal government were also to be given to the Klamath Indians.[36]

## INDIAN GRAVES AND FUNERARY OBJECTS

Native Americans, believing that they have a spiritual connection with ancestral remains, have had little success in litigating disputes about development of Indian burial grounds, removal of gravestones by developers, or malicious disturbance of Indian tombs or graves.[37] While it can be said that "only recently" have Native Americans "felt they were in a position to bring a white government to court,"[38] the more effective avenue has been through Congress.

In 1989, Congress passed legislation to establish the National Museum of the American Indian within the Smithsonian Institution. Part of the statute required the Secretary of the Smithsonian Institution, in consultation and cooperation with traditional Indian religious leaders and government officials of Indian tribes, to inventory the Indian human remains and Indian funerary objects in the possession or control of the Smithsonian Institution, and to return to the descendants or tribes the human remains and associated funerary objects that can be associated with the descendants and tribes.[39]

The following year, Congress passed the Native American Graves Protection and Repatriation Act. In reporting the bill, the House Committee

---

[34] 68 Stat. 719 (1954).
[35] H. Rept. No. 99-630, 99th Cong., 2d Sess. 3 (1986).
[36] 100 Stat. 849 (1986). For floor debate, see 132 Cong. Rec. 13753-55, 21775-76 (1986).
[37] Wana the Bear v. Community Const., Inc., 180 Cal. Rptr. 423 (Ct. App. 1982); State v. Glass, 273 N.E.2d 893 (Ohio 1971); Newman v. State, 174 So.2d 479 (Fla. 1965); Carter v. City of Zanesville, 52 N.E. 126 (Ohio 898).
[38] June Camille Bush Raines, "One Is Missing; Native American Graves Protection and Repatriation Act: An Overview and Analysis," 17 Am. Ind. L. Rev. 636, 646 (1992).
[39] 103 Stat. 1343, § 11 (1989).

on Interior and Insular Affairs explained its purpose: "To protect Native American burial sites and the removal of human remains, funerary objects, sacred objects, and objects of cultural patrimony on Federal, Indian and Native Hawaiian lands."[40] Persons who excavate or do archaeological work on federal lands must receive a permit. If any human remains or funereal objects are discovered, and it is known which tribe is closely related to them, that tribe is given the opportunity to reclaim the remains or objects. If they decide not to take possession, the Secretary of the Interior will determine the disposition after consulting with Native American, scientific, and museum groups. In previous years, Indian tribes had tried to have the human remains and funerary objects of their ancestors returned to them.[41]

The bill passed the House under suspension of the rules.[42] Representative Ben Nighthorse Campbell, whose father was Northern Cheyenne, discussed an order by the Surgeon General in 1868 to have Army field officers send him Indian skeletons. The purpose of the study, Campbell said, was to determine whether the Indian was inferior to the white man, because of a smaller cranium, and to show that the Indian was not capable of being a landowner.[43] Indian tribes wanted to recover these and other remains. The bill passed the Senate by voice vote, with little debate.[44] Differences between the two chambers were resolved with little difficulty.[45] As enacted, the legislation provides criminal penalties for those engaged in illegal trafficking in Indian human remains and cultural items.[46]

---

[40] H. Rept. No. 101-877, 101st Cong., 2d Sess. 8 (1990).
[41] Id. at 13.
[42] 136 Cong. Rec. 31941 (1990).
[43] Id. at 31937.
[44] Id. at 34061-62.
[45] Id. at 35677-91, 36814-15.
[46] 104 Stat. 3052, § 4 (1990).

*Chapter 8*

# RELIGIOUS USE OF PEYOTE

Congress as well the Oregon legislature passed legislation to authorize the use of peyote by Indians as part of a religious ceremony. Efforts to have those religious freedoms protected in court were not so successful. Two decisions by the Supreme Court, in 1990 and 1997, provoked widespread public criticism and led to remedial legislation backed by a broad coalition of religious and civil rights groups. Peyote grows in small buttons at the top of a spineless cactus and contains a number of alkaloids, including the psychotropic mescaline. With its hallucinogenic properties, peyote offers "a supernaturalistic alternative" to other religions.[1] As practiced by the Native American Church (NAC), the drug is considered a sacrament (like bread and wine) and an object of worship. By ingesting peyote, members of the NAC say they enter into direct contact with god. The House report noted that peyote is not injurious to the Indian religious user, is not addictive or habit-forming, and is often helpful in controlling alcoholism and alcohol abuse among Indian people.[2]

Initially, states and territories responded to peyote by forbidding its use. In 1899, Oklahoma prohibited use of the mescal bean but repealed the law in 1908.[3] Other states enacted legislation to prohibit the use of peyote: Colorado, Nevada, and Utah in 1917; Kansas in 1920; Arizona, Montana, North Dakota, and South Dakota in 1923; Iowa in 1924; New Mexico and Wyoming in 1929; and Texas in 1937.[4] In 1926, the Supreme Court of

---

[1] George de Verges, "Peyote and the Native American Church," 2 Am. Ind. L. Rev. 71 (1974); H. Kept. No. 103-675, 103d Cong., 2d Sess. 3 (1994).

[2] H. Rept. No. 103-675,103d Cong., 2d Sess. 3 (1994).

[3] Omar C. Stewart, "Peyote and the Law," in Christopher Vecsey, ed., Handbook on American Indian Religious Freedom 60 (1991).

[4] De Verges, "Peyote and the Native American Church," 2 Am. Ind. L, Rev. at 77 n.14.

Montana held that under some circumstances the state could enforce the state law prohibiting peyote against an Indian who used it within a reservation.[5]

Several congressional statutes in the nineteenth century had prohibited the sale of intoxicating drinks to Indians.[6] Lawmakers made an effort in 1913 to provide funds to suppress the use of peyote, but conferees deleted the money, explaining that "the Indians claim this peyote is used in their religious worship and would cause a great deal of confusion."[7] The enacted bill did not contain money to suppress peyote.[8]

In 1918, the House Committee on Indian Affairs reported legislation to prohibit the sale of peyote to Indians. The committee, accepting the recommendation of the Indian Bureau and relying on published articles, described peyote as "poison" and referred to "night orgies in a close [sic] tent polluted with foul air."[9] The bureau noted that peyote was used by Indians "as a substitute for intoxicating liquors," but accepted that evidence as a ground to prohibit the use of peyote.[10]

The committee acted in this manner because the peyote bill was caught up in the national campaign for prohibition in general, eventually leading to ratification of the Eighteenth Amendment in 1919. Even so, the committee report includes an encyclopedia article that describes peyote as "producing a pleasant dreaminess without, however, overmastering the will power," and states that peyote "effectively checks tendencies toward alcoholism."[11]

The House passed the committee-reported bill to prohibit the sale of intoxicating liquor, Indian hemp, or peyote to any Indian. An amendment to permit the sale of peyote when used for religious purposes was rejected, and the bill as a whole passed.[12] The Senate took no action on this House bill. Instead, it debated an amendment to prohibit the introduction of peyote into Indian territories. The amendment was rejected on a point of order because it constituted general legislation on an appropriations bill.[13] Although this bill did not pass, Interior Department appropriations acts from 1923 to 1934 contained funds to suppress "the traffic in intoxicating liquors and deleterious drugs, including peyote, among Indians."[14]

---

[5] State v. Big Sheep, 242 P. 1067 (Mont. 1926).
[6] E.g., 4 Stat. 732, § 20 (1834) and 29 Stat. 506 (1897).
[7] H. Rept. No. 28, 63d Cong., 1st Sess. 6 (1913).
[8] 38 Stat. 78 (1913).
[9] H. Rept. No. 560, 65th Cong., 2d Sess. 26 (1918).
[10] Id. at 2.
[11] Id. at 11.
[12] 56 Cong. Rec. 11113-15 (1918).
[13] Id. at 4129-33.
[14] 42 Stat. 1182 (1923); 43 Stat. 396 (1924); 43 Stat. 1147 (1925); 44 Stat. 458 (1926); 44 Stat. 939 (1927); 45 Stat. 204 (1928); 45 Stat. 1566 (1929); 46 Stat. 1119 (1931); 47 Stat. 94

## REFORM MOVEMENT

Montana in 1957 and New Mexico in 1959 amended their narcotic laws to provide that the prohibition against narcotics "shall not apply to the possession, sale or gift of peyote for religious sacramental purposes by a bona fide religious organization incorporated under the laws of the state."[15] During this period, a federal appellate court left standing an ordinance adopted by the Navajo Tribal Council making it an offense to introduce peyote into Navajo country. The Navajos entered the house of an NAC member during the conduct of religious ceremonies. The court held that in the absence of a constitutional provision or a congressional statute making the Bill of Rights applicable to Indian nations, federal courts lacked jurisdiction over tribal laws or regulations.[16]

In 1960, an Arizona trial court ruled against the state in a case involving a Navajo woman arrested for illegal possession of peyote. The court held that her religious interests outweighed whatever governmental interest the state could present. The state appealed, but the Arizona Supreme Court affirmed the holding of the trial judge.[17]

Several years later, in 1964, the California Supreme Court reached a similar result in *People v. Woody*. State police had arrested a group of Navajos who used peyote during a religious ceremony. The court ruled that since the defendants used peyote "in a bona fide pursuit of a religious faith," and since there was no compelling state interest to override that use, application of the statute in this instance violated the First Amendment. Although the First Amendment was not applicable to Indian nations (and would not be until 1968), it applied to the states.[18]

Two years after this case, a California trial court rejected an individual's argument that he had a religious right to plant, cultivate, and smoke marijuana. He was not a member of any organized religion. What he called religion was his own personal philosophy and way of life, unlike the religious practices of the Native American Church and the established use of peyote as a sacrament.[19] In 1969, a California appellate court upheld the

---

(1932); 47 Stat. 824 (1933); 48 Stat. 366 (1934). Funds for peyote suppression was not included in the 1935 Interior appropriations bill; 49 Stat. 162 (1935).

[15] People v. Woody, 394 P.2d 813, 819 (Cal. 1964).

[16] Native American Church v. Navajo Tribal Council, 272 F.2d 131 (10th Cir. 1959).

[17] Neither decision in this case, Arizona v. Attakai, Criminal No. 4098, Coconino County, was reported, but it is cited in People v. Woody, 394 P.2d at 813 n.5; see Carolyn N. Long, Religious Freedom and Indian Rights 18 (2000).

[18] People v. Woody, 394 P.2d at 815.

[19] People v. Mitchell, 52 Cal.Rptr. 884, 886-87 (1966).

conviction of someone who said he used marijuana "for meditative communication with the Supreme Being." The court found no similarity between the use of marijuana in this case and the NAC's use of peyote as part of a formalized religious practice.[20]

Other cases decided during this period went against the use of drugs for supposedly religious reasons. A North Carolinian who called himself a Peyotist with Buddhist leanings" and a member of the Neo-American Church (unrelated to the Native American Church) claimed that his use of peyote and marijuana was protected by the First Amendment. The North Carolina Supreme Court did not agree.[21] In 1968, a federal court rejected the argument of a Neo-American Church member who claimed that her ingestion of marijuana and LSD was required for a religious experience. Her case involved more than the personal use of drugs; she was also indicted for unlawful sale and delivery.[22]

None of these cases challenged *Woody's* support for using peyote in a religious ceremony conducted by the NAC. In 1972, a state appellate court in Arizona upheld the use of peyote in a religious ceremony (a wedding) convened by the Native American Church. Peyotism, said the court, "is not a twentieth century cult nor a fad subject to extinction at a whim."[23] In deciding a peyote case in 1974, the Ninth Circuit accepted much of *Woody* without actually embracing it as federal law.[24]

Going against these cases was an Oregon decision in 1975. The state police, after arresting an individual for failure to have a driver's license, discovered peyote during a search. Convicted of unlawfully possessing mescaline, or peyote, he was not given an opportunity to present evidence of his religious beliefs or his membership in the Native American Church. The Court of Appeals of Oregon affirmed his conviction.[25] Two years later, an Oklahoma appellate court held that the state had failed to show a compelling interest in preventing NAC members from possessing and transporting peyote within the state as a religious symbol.[26]

---

[20] People v. Collins, 78 Cal.Rptr. 151, 152 (1969).
[21] State v. Bullard, 148 S.E.2d 565 (N.C. 1966).
[22] United States v. Kuch, 288 F.Supp. 439 (D.D.C. 1968).
[23] State v. Whittingham, 504 P.2d 950, 952 (Ariz. 1972).
[24] Golden Eagle v. Johnson, 493 F.2d 1179, 1183 (9th Or. 1974).
[25] State v. Soto, 537 P.2d 142 (Ore. 1975), cert. denied, 424 U.S. 955 (1976).
[26] Whitehorn v. State, 561 P.2d 539 (Okla. 1977). See Robert Johnston, "Whitehorn v. State: Peyote and Religious Freedom in Oklahoma," 5 Am. Ind. L. Rev. 229 (1977).

## FEDERAL CONTROLS

Beginning in the 1960s, the federal government took action to secure the religious use of peyote by NAC members. In passing a drug abuse act in 1965, Congress left to the executive branch broad discretion in making exemptions for depressant or stimulant drugs. The House bill had provided the NAC with a specific exemption for peyote, but the Senate — and the enacted bill — left that issue to administrative regulation.[27]

The following year, the Commissioner of Food and Drugs listed a number of drugs that had a depressant effect on the central nervous system, including mescaline and its salts and peyote. The notice in the *Federal Register* explains that the listing of peyote "does not apply to non-drug use in bona fide religious ceremonies of the Native American Church; however, persons supplying the product to the Church are required to register and maintain appropriate records of receipts and disbursements of the article."[28]

Several churches, wanting to use peyote in their religious ceremonies, challenged the special exemption for NAC members. The Church of the Awakening, a non-Indian religious body, asked a federal court to add its name in the *Code of Federal Regulations* along with the NAC. In 1972, the Ninth Circuit acknowledged that the federal regulation was arbitrary in classifying the NAC one way and other churches another way, but said it would be equally arbitrary to place the NAC and the Church of the Awakening in one category and all other churches in another.[29]

In 1978, the Drug Enforcement Agency (DEA) of the Justice Department issued a notice to discuss implementation of a federal regulation that specifically exempted NAC members from the registration requirement — under the Controlled Substances Act — for the use of peyote in bona fide religious ceremonies.[30] The purpose of the notice was not to rescind or reduce the exemption, but rather to discuss the difficulty of identifying bona fide church members and to search for ways of preventing unauthorized persons from taking advantage of the exemption. In 1981, the Office of Legal Counsel (OLC) of the Justice Department released an opinion expressing its view that the DEA regulation exempting peyote use in

---

[27] 111 Cong. Rec. 14608 (1965); 79 Stat. 226 (1965).
[28] 31 Fed. Reg. 4679 (1966); the peyote exception for the NAC currently appears in 21 C.F.R. § 1307.31 (4-1-01 ed.).
[29] Kennedy v. Bureau of Narcotics and Dangerous Drugs, 459 F.2d 415 (9th Cir. 1972).
[30] 43 Fed. Reg. 56106 (1978).

connection with NAC religious ceremonies accurately reflected congressional intent.[31]

In 1984, the Fifth Circuit received another challenge to the special exemption, this time from the Peyote Way Church of God. The court remanded the case to the district court to determine whether the federal regulation denied religious freedom to the Peyote Way Church.[32] When the case returned, the Fifth Circuit upheld the special exemption for the NAC on the grounds that Congress had been given extraordinary authority over Indian matters and the special exemption was rationally related to the legitimate governmental objective of preserving Indian culture.[33]

In 1979, a federal district court in New York read the peyote exception differently. In addition to the NAC, it ruled that the exception covered the Native American Church of New York, which was not affiliated with the NAC, and only a few of its roughly one thousand members were Indians. Also, the Native American Church of New York expresses a belief that all psychedelic drugs, including LSD and marijuana, are deities.[34] The district court concluded that the exemption for peyote is available to any bona fide religious organization that uses peyote for sacramental purposes and regards peyote as a deity.[35]

## THE ALFRED SMITH CASE

Alfred Smith, a Klamath Indian and member of the NAC, had served as a counselor for alcoholics since 1971. He worked for ADAPT (Alcohol and Drug Abuse Prevention and Treatment) in Oregon from August 25, 1982, until his discharge on March 5, 1984. ADAPT required counselors to abstain from alcohol and mind-altering drugs and warned Smith that he could be discharged for using peyote, even if part of a religious ceremony. After ingesting peyote during a weekend service conducted by the NAC, Smith was fired and subsequently denied unemployment benefits because of the drug use.[36]

In 1986, the Supreme Court of Oregon held that while the denial of benefits did not violate state constitutional provisions regarding freedom of

---

[31] 5 Ops. Off. Legal Counsel 403 (1981).
[32] Peyote Way Church of God, Inc. v. Smith, 742 F.2d 193 (5th Cir. 1984).
[33] Peyote Way Church of God, Inc. v. Thornburgh, 922 F.2d 1210, 1216 (5th Cir. 1991).
[34] Native American Church of New York v. United States, 468 F.Supp. 1247, 1248 (S.D.N.Y. 1979), aff'd, 633 F.2d 205 (2d Cir. 1980).
[35] Native American Church of New York v. United States, 468 F.Supp. at 1251.
[36] Smith v. Employment Div., 721 P.2d 445, 445-46 (Ore. 1986).

worship and religious opinion, it did violate the Free Exercise Clause of the First Amendment of the U.S. Constitution.[37] It relied on the standards announced in 1963 by the U.S. Supreme Court in *Sherbert* v. *Verner:* the person claiming the free exercise right must show that the application of law "significantly burdens" the free exercise of religion, and the state must show that the constraint on religious liberty is the "least restrictive" means of achieving a "compelling" state interest.[38] A companion case before the Oregon Supreme Court involved Galen Black, a non-Indian who belonged to the NAC. He was also denied unemployment benefits after being fired for ingesting peyote during a religious ceremony.

Under Oregon law, the possession of peyote was a crime. Unemployment benefits could be denied when an employee was discharged for misconduct, in this case by ingesting peyote. Although the state defended the law as part of its general policy against drug use, the Oregon Supreme Court held that the state had not shown that the financial stability of the unemployment insurance fund would be "imperiled by claimants applying for religious exemptions if this claimant receives benefits."[39]

The Attorney General of Oregon appealed the case to the U.S. Supreme Court. In 1988, the Court vacated the Oregon ruling and returned the case with the request that the Oregon Supreme Court decide whether the religious use of peyote was legal in that state. The U.S. Supreme Court pointed out that the results reached in *Sherbert* and other unemployment cases "might well have been different if the employees had been discharged for engaging in criminal conduct."[40] Passages in the decision seemed to suggest that Oregon could deny unemployment benefits to Smith and Galen.[41]

The Oregon Supreme Court reaffirmed its earlier ruling by holding that the First Amendment entitled Smith and Black to their unemployment benefits. The state court pointed out that when Congress passed the Drug Abuse Control Amendments of 1965, for the purpose of bringing peyote under federal control, it expected the implementing regulation to exempt the religious use of peyote by the NAC. In 1970 and 1978, Congress passed additional legislation offering support for the use of peyote in religious ceremonies.[42] As anticipated by Congress, the implementing regulation

---

[37] Id. at 446-49.
[38] Id. at 449.
[39] Id. at 451.
[40] Employment Division v. Smith, 485 U.S. 660, 671 (1988).
[41] Id. ("If a bigamist may be sent to jail despite the religious motivation for his misconduct, surely a State may refuse to pay unemployment compensation to a marriage counselor who was discharged because he or she entered into a bigamous relationship.")
[42] Smith v. Employment Division, 763 P.2d 146, 149 (Ore. 1988).

issued in 1971 stated that the listing of peyote as a controlled substance" does not apply to the nondrug use of peyote in bona fide religious ceremonies of the Native American Church."[43]

The Attorney General of Oregon again urged the U.S. Supreme Court to review this latest decision of the Oregon Supreme Court. He objected strongly to the reliance by the state supreme court on congressional interpretations of the Constitution:

> The Oregon Supreme Court's holding is not a product of the court's independent assessment of what the first amendment requires. At most, it represents a choice to defer to congressional assumptions about the requirements of the federal constitution.... This process of canvassing congressional understanding to resolve an important first amendment question would be troubling under any circumstance.[44]

The Attorney General of Oregon defended the state's interest in controlling drugs. Few regulatory areas, he said, invoke governmental interest in public health and safety "with force equal to that of drug use." Few drugs trigger that interest "with strength equal to that of hallucinogens, such as peyote."[45] Although some state courts had held that the federal Free Exercise Clause protects the use of peyote to NAC members, he pointed to contrary rulings by the Oregon courts.[46]

By the time the case returned to the U.S. Supreme Court, some of the original conditions had changed substantially to raise the question of whether the dispute was still a live controversy. For example, as part of a federal consent decree, ADAPT agreed that the religious use of peyote by NAC members would no longer be considered work-related misconduct. The conditions that led to the denial of benefits to Smith and Black could not arise again in Oregon.[47] Also, Smith and Black won back pay.[48] Other factors pointed to mootness. Smith and Black exhausted the unemployment benefits they received as a result of the first decision by the Oregon Supreme Court; under Oregon law they could not be forced to repay the benefits even

---

[43] 21 C.F.R. § 1307.31.
[44] Petition for Writ of Certiorari to the Supreme Court of the State of Oregon, Employment Division v. Smith; 196 Landmark Briefs 425.
[45] Id. at 426.
[46] Brief for Petitioners, Employment Division v. Smith; 196 Landmark Briefs 478 n.26, citing State v. Soto, 537 P.2d 142 (Ore. 1975), cert. denied, 424 U.S. 955 (1976), upholding the prohibition of mescaline even for religious purposes.
[47] Brief in Opposition to Petition for Writ of Certiorari, Employment Division v. Smith; 196 Landmark Briefs 2.
[48] Garrett Epps, "To an Unknown God: The Hidden History of *Employment Division* v. *Smith*," 30 Ariz. St. L. J. 953, 989 (1998).

if the second decision of the state court was reversed by the U.S. Supreme Court; and the time period for charging Smith and Black with violating Oregon's drug laws had passed.[49] The Attorney General of Oregon disputed some of these points, claiming that there was still time for the state to collect the benefits from Smith and Black.[50]

In 1990, the U.S. Supreme Court attempted to settle the matter by holding that the Free Exercise Clause permits a state to prohibit sacramental peyote use and to deny unemployment benefits to persons discharged for such use. The Court ruled that state law may prohibit the possession and use of a drug even if it incidentally prohibits a religious practice, provided that the state law is neutral and generally applicable to all individuals.[51] Under this test, there was no need for the state to show a compelling interest or to use the least restrictive means. The Court therefore abandoned the *Sherbert* standard.

Immediately after the Court's decision, a broad coalition of religious groups sought a rehearing in the case. They argued that the new standard developed by the Court would require a "massive reordering of the delicate relationship between individuals and religious organizations and the power of the state."[52] The Court denied the motion for a rehearing.[53]

With judicial relief less available, interest groups turned to legislative remedies in Congress and Oregon. A bill introduced in Congress in 1990, the Religious Freedom Restoration Act (RFRA), was drafted to reinstate the Sherbert standard for protecting religious freedom. While Congress considered this bill, the Oregon legislature enacted a bill that protected the sacramental use of peyote by NAC. The enacted bill states that in any prosecution for the manufacture, possession, or delivery of peyote, it is an affirmative defense that the peyote is being used or is intended for use (1) in connection with the good faith practice of a religious belief, (2) as directly associated with a religious practice, and (3) in a manner that is not dangerous to the health of the user or others who are in the proximity of the user.[54]

At the hearings on RFRA, scholars and lobbyists testified strongly that Congress had a right and a duty to act when the Court endangers fundamental freedoms. Robert Dugan, Jr., representing the National

---

[49] Brief for Respondents, Employment Division v. Smith; 196 Landmark Briefs 542.
[50] Reply Brief for Petitioners, Employment Division v. Smith; 196 Landmark Briefs 552.
[51] Employment Division v. Smith, 494 U.S. 872 (1990).
[52] "High Court Urged to Reconsider," Washington Post, May 12, 1990, at C11. See also "Hail Mary Pass," Legal Times, May 14, 1990, at 11.
[53] Employment Division v. Smith, 496 U.S. 913 (1990).
[54] Oregon Laws, Chap. 329, § 1 (June 24, 1991), reprinted in 1995 Oregon Revised Statutes, 475.992, § 5 (v. 9, p. 80).

Association of Evangelicals, said that the Court, intended to be a guardian of constitutional freedoms, has "deprived us of our birthright as Americans" and emptied the Free Exercise Clause of its meaning. The system of checks and balances, he said, empowered Congress "to overrule the Court by restoring the compelling interest test."[55] Dallin H. Oaks, from the Mormon Church, regarded the statutory restoration of the compelling interest standard as "both a legitimate and a necessary response by the legislative branch to the degradation of religious freedom resulting from the Smith case."[56] Nadine Strossen of the ACLU appealed to Congress to act: "The Supreme Court has cast us back into the good graces of this legislature, and it does depend on you, our elected representatives, to restore to all of us the religious freedom that should be protected by the Constitution but that the U.S. Supreme Court has refused to protect that way. Please restore our religious liberty through legislation."[57] At Senate hearings, one witness called *Smith* "the Dred Scott of first amendment law."[58]

The House Judiciary Committee reported RFRA in 1993, voting 35 to zero. The bill was designed to require the compelling governmental interest test in cases in which the free exercise of religion has been burdened by a law of general applicability.[59] The legislation did not mandate states to permit the ceremonial use of peyote; it merely subjected any prohibition to the compelling interest test.[60] The bill passed the House under suspension of the rules.[61]

The Senate Judiciary Committee, voting 15 to 1, reported RFRA for floor consideration.[62] By the time the bill headed for final passage, 68 religious and civil liberties groups were lined up behind it.[63] On final passage, the bill passed 97 to 3.[64] As enacted, RFRA provided that governments may substantially burden a person's religious exercise only if they demonstrate a compelling interest and use the least restrictive means of furthering that interest. The term "government" applied to any branch,

---

[55] "Religious Freedom Restoration Act of 1991," hearings before the House Committee on the Judiciary, 102d Cong., 2d Sess. 10, 14 (1992).
[56] Id. at 25.
[57] Id. at 64-65.
[58] "The Religious Freedom Restoration Act," hearing before the Senate Committee on the Judiciary, 102d Cong., 2d Sess. 42 (1992); Oliver S. Thomas, general counsel, Baptist Joint Committee on Public Affairs.
[59] H. Rept. No. 103-88,103d Cong., 1st Sess. 1-2 (1993).
[60] Id. at 7.
[61] 139 Cong. Rec. 9680-87 (1993).
[62] S. Rept. No. 103-11, 103d Cong., 1st Sess. (1993).
[63] "Disparate Groups Unite Behind Civil Rights Bill on Religious Freedom," Washington Post, October 16, 1993, at A7.
[64] 139 Cong. Rec. 26416 (1993).

department, agency, instrumentality, or official at the federal, state, and local level.[65]

A year later, Congress passed legislation to permit the use of peyote by Native Americans during religious ceremonies.[66] As Senator Paul Wellstone remarked, leaving the definition of standards for religious freedom "up to the judiciary has not proved very effective for native American religions."[67] Patrick H. Lefthand, a member of the Kootenai tribe, told the Senate Committee on Indian Affairs that the Supreme Court decided that "our religion did not deserve the same protection afforded to all Americans who practice Judeo-Christian religions," and urged Congress to pass legislation "to ensure the continuation and vitality of Indian communities."[68]

DEA officials testified that the religious use of peyote by Indians had nothing to do with the vast and violent traffic in illegal narcotics in the United States. The DEA was also unaware of the diversion of peyote to any illicit market.[69] The bill enacted in 1994 specifically recognizes that "for many Indian people, the traditional ceremonial use of the peyote cactus as a religious sacrament has for centuries been integral to a way of life, and significant in perpetuating Indian tribes and cultures."[70] The statute also notes that the Supreme Court's decision in *Smith* did not protect Indian practitioners who used peyote in Indian religious ceremonies.[71]

## RFRA INVALIDATED

In 1997, the Supreme Court ruled that Congress exceeded the scope of its enforcement power under Section 5 of the Fourteenth Amendment by applying RFRA to the states.[72] A separate question concerned the constitutionality of RFRA as applied not to the states but to the federal government. In 1998, the Eighth Circuit held that RFRA was constitutional as applied to federal law, it did not violate the separation of powers doctrine,

---

[65] 107 Stat. 1488 (1993).
[66] 108 Stat. 3125 (1994).
[67] 139 Cong. Rec. 10971 (1993).
[68] "Native American Free Exercise of Religious Freedom Act," hearing before the Senate Committee on Indian Affairs, 103d Cong., 2d Sess. 98-99 (1993).
[69] H. Rept. No. 103-675, 103d Cong., 2d Sess. 4 (1994).
[70] 108 Stat. 3125, § 2 (amending the American Indian Religious Freedom Act of 1878 by adding section 3(a)(l)).
[71] Id., § 3(a)(4).
[72] Boerne v. Flores, 521 U.S. 507 (1997). For legal analysis of this decision, see David M. Ackerman, "The Religious Freedom Restoration Act: Its Rise, Fall, and Current Status," CRS Report 97-795 A (January 21, 1999).

and it did not violate the Establishment Clause.[73] In 2001, the Tenth Circuit ruled that RFRA was a legitimate congressional action under Article I to govern the conduct of federal prison officials.[74]

Following the invalidation of RFRA, the House Judiciary Committee held hearings to consider alternative legislation. Representative Robert Scott said that RFRA could be reconfigured by relying on the Interstate Commerce Clause or the Spending Clause.[75] The Senate Judiciary Committee also held hearings to explore the legislative options available to Congress.[76] The following year, Senator Orrin Hatch introduced the Religious Liberty Protection Act (RLPA) to respond to *Boerne*. He relied primarily on the commerce and spending powers.[77] A similar bill, which passed the House in 1999, was supported by 92 religious and civil liberties groups.[78] The bill passed the House by a vote of 306 to 118.[79]

By the time the bill cleared both chambers in 2000, it had been restricted to provide two kinds of protections. First, it offered religious groups protection in land-use disputes, such as zoning issues (the kind that triggered *Boerne*). Second, the statute makes it easier for prisoners and other persons confined in state-run institutions to practice their faith. The statute applies to any organization that receives federal money, including state and local prisons that get federal construction and maintenance funds. Finally, the statute relies on congressional power over interstate commerce, because

---

[73] In re Young, 141 F.3d 854 (8th Cir. 1998), cert, denied, sub nom. Christians, Trustee v. Crystal Evangelical Free Church, 525 U.S. 811 (1998).
[74] Kikumura v. Hurley, 242 F.3d 950 (10th Cir. 2001).
[75] "Protecting Religious Freedom After Boerne v. Flores," hearing before the House Committee on the Judiciary, 105th cong., 1st Sess. 2 (1997).
[76] "Congress' Constitutional Role in Protecting Religious Liberty," hearings before the Senate Committee on the Judiciary, 105th Cong., 1st Sess. (1997).
[77] 144 Cong. Rec. S5791 (daily ed. June 9, 1998).
[78] 145 Cong. Rec. H5583 (daily ed. July 15, 1999).
[79] Id. at H5608.

construction materials are shipped between states for the renovation of buildings owned by religious organizations.[80]

---

[80] 114 Stat. 803 (2000).

*Chapter 9*

# STATUTORY EXEMPTIONS

Earlier sections of this report described statutory exemptions for religious purposes in such areas as conscientious objectors, religious apparel in the military, and the religious use of peyote. Other exemptions are covered in this section: religious exemptions for property and income taxes, the exception for sacramental wine in prohibition statutes, legislation that excused the Amish from paying Social Security taxes, exceptions for religious organizations in statutes that prohibit discrimination, and an exception in the Humane Slaughter Act for religious dietary laws. Each statute required Congress to evaluate the religious values of different organizations and devise accommodations consistent with the Free Exercise and Establishment Clauses.

## TAX EXEMPTIONS

From early colonial times, churches received tax exemptions for their property. Critics of this assistance regard it as an indirect state subsidy in violation of the Establishment Clause, but efforts to tax church property would trigger the objection that the government is attempting to interfere with the free exercise of religion. Courts recognize that legislatures may adjust their systems of taxation to provide exemptions for property owned by religious organizations.[1] To the extent that programs operated by religious

---

[1] Bell's Gap R.R. v. Pennsylvania, 134 U.S. 232, 237 (1890); Washington Ethical Society v. District of Columbia, 249 F.2d 127, 129 (D.C. Cir. 1957). See Arvo Van Alstyne, "Tax Exemption of Church Properly," 20 Ohio State L. J. 461, 462 n.6 (1959).

institutions promote social benefits, it can be argued that they relieve the public of burdens that would have to be met by general taxation.[2]

For religious organizations, the exemption for property taxes can cover places of religious worship (both church buildings and adjacent land), living quarters for clergy (parsonages), cemeteries, church-affiliated schools and colleges, and such charitable properties as hospitals, orphanages, homes for the aged, asylums, poorhouses, and missionary societies.[3] Courts often have to determine whether a religious organization is qualified to receive property tax exemption. Otherwise, ordinary citizens could escape taxation by claiming some religious purpose.[4]

Although exemption from property taxes is primarily a matter of state law, the Supreme Court has examined congressional statutes to determine the extent to which church lands are exempt from taxation.[5] In 1970, the Court decided the constitutionality of property tax exemptions for religious organizations. A plaintiff argued that the tax exemption for religious purposes, included in the New York Constitution, created an establishment of religion prohibited by the First Amendment. The Court, pointing out that all 50 states provided for tax exemptions for places of worship and that a number of federal statutes granted tax exemptions for churches, denied that these state and federal practices either "established" religion or reasonably threatened to do so.[6]

Beginning in 1894, Congress provided that the federal income tax did not apply to corporations "conducted solely for charitable, religious, or educational purposes."[7] After the Supreme Court in *Pollock* v. *Farmer's Loan and Trust Co.* (1895) struck down the federal income tax, Congress responded with the Sixteenth Amendment to empower Congress to tax incomes. Federal income tax statutes after that time stipulated that the tax did not apply to any corporation or association "organized and operated exclusively for religious, charitable, scientific, or educational purposes."[8] This exemption today appears in Section 501(c)(3) of the Internal Revenue Code.

---

[2] 3 Stokes 419.
[3] Van Alstyne, "Tax Exemptions of Church Property," 20 Ohio State L. J. at 463-64, 470, 479, 484, 490, 496-97.
[4] For example, Golden Writ of God v. Dept. of Rev., 713 P.2d 605 (Ore. 1986).
[5] Gibbons v. District of Columbia, 116 U.S. 404 (1886).
[6] Walz v. Tax Commission, 397 U.S. 664, 676-78 (1970).
[7] 28 Stat. 556 (1894).
[8] 38 Stat. 172 (1913). See also 40 Stat. 330 (1917) and 40 Stat. 1076, § 231(6) (1919).

## PROHIBITION STATUTES

From 1912 to 1919, Congress passed a number of statutes and constitutional amendments to prohibit the manufacture and selling of intoxicating beverages. Each time it made exception for the use of sacramental wines for religious ceremonies. Legislation in 1912, designed to suppress the traffic of intoxicating liquors among Indians, made it lawful to introduce and use wines "solely for sacramental purposes, under church authority."[9] A proposed constitutional amendment introduced in 1913 would have prohibited intoxicating beverages but gave Congress the power to provide for the manufacture and sale of intoxicating liquors for certain exceptions, including sacramental purposes.[10] The proposal, attracting committee and floor interest, failed to pass either chamber.[11] The Webb-Kenyon Act of 1913 prohibited the shipment of intoxicating liquors into a state in violation of its laws.[12] Although the statute made no mention of sacramental wine, legislators understood that virtually every state allowed wines to be used for sacramental purposes.[13]

Federal legislation enacted on February 14, 1917, prohibited the manufacture or sale of alcoholic liquors in the Territory of Alaska. Although the bill debated by Congress was described as "a bone-dry bill,"[14] designed to totally prohibit the consumption of alcohol, the bill as introduced made an exception for sacramental wine. The bill's language seemed confined to the use of communion wine by Christians.[15] The bill, including the exception for sacramental wine, was enacted.[16] Also in 1917, Congress prohibited the mailing of any letter, postal card, circular, newspaper, pamphlet, or publication from containing any advertisement of "spirituous, vinous, malted, fermented, or other intoxicating liquors of any kind." Individuals would be punished for ordering, purchasing, or transporting intoxicating liquors, but an exception was carved out "for scientific, sacramental, medicinal, and mechanical purposes."[17] The general term "sacramental" was

---

[9] 37 Stat. 519 (1912).
[10] 51 Cong. Rec. 615 (1913).
[11] Richard F. Hamm, Shaping the Eighteenth Amendment: Temperance Reform, Legal Culture, and the Polity, 1880-1920, at 228-29 (1995).
[12] 37 Stat. 699 (1913).
[13] 54 Cong. Rec. 3396 (1917) (exchange between Senators Vardaman, Kenyon, and Reed).
[14] Id. at 2530.
[15] S. 7963, 64th Cong., 2d Sess. 6 (1917) (referring to "a duly authorized and officiating priest or minister").
[16] 39 Stat. 905, § 8 (1917).
[17] 39 Stat. 1069, § 5 (1917).

broad enough to cover not only communion wine used by Christians but also wine consumed at dinner during a Jewish Seder.

World War I placed great strains on the national economy. In an effort to help in the prosecution of the war, Congress passed legislation in 1918 to prohibit the use of any grains, cereals, fruit, or other food products for the manufacture of beer, wine, "or other intoxicating malt or vinous for beverage purposes." No beer, wine, or other intoxicating malt or vinous liquor could be sold for beverage purposes except for export.[18] The government was authorized to prescribe rules and regulations regarding the manufacture and sale of distilled spirits and for the manufacture, sale, and distribution of wine for "sacramental, medicinal, or other than beverage use."[19]

Finally, the National Prohibition Act of 1919 (the Volstead Act) prohibited intoxicating beverages and regulated the manufacture, production, use, and sale of high-proof spirits intended for other than beverage purposes. It prohibited any person after the Eighteenth Amendment took effect (January 16, 1919) from manufacturing, selling, bartering, transporting, importing, exporting, delivering, furnishing or possessing any intoxicating liquor. However, an exception was made for liquor in the form of "wine for sacramental purposes," subject to government regulation.[20] The bill language referred to ministers, priests, and rabbis.[21]

## EXEMPTIONS FROM SOCIAL SECURITY

Congress has exempted some members of religious orders from paying into the Social Security trust fund if their religious principles are opposed to accepting social security benefits. Any individual who is a duly ordained, commissioned, or licensed minister of a church or a minister of a religious order may qualify. The exemption also covers Christian Science practitioners. These individuals may apply for the exemption by stating that they are conscientiously opposed to, or because of religious principles opposed to, the acceptance of payments from a public insurance program.[22] Moreover, any member of a "recognized religious sect or division thereof"

---

[18] 40 Stat. 1046 (1918).
[19] Id. at 1047.
[20] 41 Stat. 308, § 3 (1919).
[21] 58 Cong. Rec. 2968, 4843 (1919); H. Rept. No. 360, 66th Cong. 1st Sess. 5 (1919); 58 Cong. Rec. 6432, 6550, 6687 (1919); 41 Stat. 311 (1919).
[22] 26 U.S.C. § 1402(e) (2000).

who believes that their tenets oppose the acceptance of payments in the event of death, disability, old age, or retirement may also file for the exemption.[23]

The Amish encounter with Social Security began in 1955, when the program was first extended to cover self-employed farmers. The IRS, in an effort to collect the Social Security payroll from the Amish, seized and sold the farm animals of Amish who refused to pay into Social Security. Newspaper editorials condemned these actions by the government.[24] According to one historian, neither the IRS nor the Department of Health, Education, and Welfare was sympathetic to the religious position of the Amish on Social Security payments.[25]

Congress added the Social Security exemption for members of a religious group in 1965. The House Ways and Means Committee explained that the exemption should be one of individual choice rather than applied to an entire group. To exclude all members "would not take account of the variances in individual beliefs within any religious group, and would deny social security protection to those individuals who want it."[26] That policy was enacted into law.[27]

The scope of that exemption reached the Supreme Court in 1982. The plaintiff, a member of the Old Order Amish, employed several other Amish to work on his farm and in his carpentry shop. He failed to file Social Security tax returns required of employers, did not withhold Social Security taxes from his employees, and did not pay the employer's share of Social Security taxes. He believed that the Amish religion makes the community responsible for its members, including those dependent on assistance. He cited the Biblical injunction: "But if any provide not... for those of his own house, he hath denied the faith, and is worse than in infidel" (1 Timothy 5:6).[28] Members of the Old Amish Order "consider it a sin against God to pay money into the Social Security System, either directly through their employer or by themselves."[29]

A district court held that any law requiring the plaintiff to pay Social Security and unemployment insurance taxes was unconstitutional because it

---

[23] Id. at § 1402(g).
[24] Peter J. Ferrara, "Social Security and Taxes," in Donald B. Kraybill, ed., The Amish and the State 132 (1993).
[25] Id. at 132-37.
[26] H. Rept. No. 213, 89th Cong., 1st Sess. 102 (1965); the same language appears in S. Rept. No. 404 (Part 1), 89th Cong., 1st Sess. 116 (1965).
[27] 79 Stat. 390, § 319 (1965). For floor statements supporting this provision, see 111 Cong. Rec. 2665-66 (Rep. Gross) and 15903 (Senator Scott) (1965).
[28] Joint Appendix, United States v. Lee, No. 80-767, U.S. Supreme Court, October Term, 1980, at 22.
[29] Id. at 23.

would violate the religious belief of the Amish that they are morally obligated to provide for their own elderly and needy. The district court concluded that the loss of revenue from this grant of exemption "would be negligible" because the Old Order Amish group was clearly defined and small in number.[30] The Supreme Court held that the exemption provided by Congress applied only to self-employed individuals, not to all employers and employees who are Amish.[31] The Court argued that the nationwide Social Security system depended on mandatory participation to make it financially viable, and that it would be a "contradiction in terms" to manage the program and allow for voluntary participation.[32] At issue, however, was not a nationwide Social Security system supported by volunteers but rather an exception for the Amish. The Court asked what would happen to the federal income tax if religious adherents, believing that war is a sin, could withhold a portion of their taxes devoted to war-related activities.[33] In a concurrence, Justice Stevens nonetheless asserted that the Court "overstates the magnitude of this risk because the Amish claim applies only to a small religious community with an established welfare system of its own."[34]

Congressional testimony in 1987 put the financial risk in context. The Amish population at that time was about ninety thousand. With about 50 percent of that number representing children under sixteen and with 99 percent of Amish women not seeking employment outside the home, the male workforce was approximately twelve thousand.[35] Had the Court recognized a broader exemption, it was likely that more money would go into the Social Security fund that would be taken out. If an Amish employee worked for an Amish employer, neither would contribute to the fund and neither would accept anything from it. However, if an Amish employee worked for a non-Amish employer, the employer would be required to withhold Social Security but the Amish employee would never withdraw any fund from Social Security.[36]

As for the Court's warning that taxpayers might refuse to pay for government activities they deplore, such as war, that was never an issue in the litigation. Amish follow the biblical admonition to pay taxes and accept

---

[30] Lee v. United States Government, 497 F.Supp. 180, 182-83 (W.D. Pa. 1980).
[31] United States v. Lee, 455 U.S. 252, 256 (1982).
[32] Id. at 258.
[33] Id. at 260.
[34] Id. at 262.
[35] "Social Security Coverage of Amish Workers," hearing before the House Committee on Ways and Means, 100th cong., 1st Sess. 11-12 (1987).
[36] Id. at 14.

the division between God and Caesar. What tax money "is used for is not our concern but the Government's."[37] Amish object to Social Security not because it is a tax but because it is an old-age insurance program that conflicts with their religious beliefs.[38]

Finding the Court's interpretation too narrow, Congress enacted legislation that broadened the exemption for the Amish. As part of the Tax Reform Act of 1988, Congress exempted employers and employees from paying social security taxes when they are members of religious faiths opposed to participation in Social Security Act programs. To qualify for this exemption, employers and employees file applications with the Department of Health and Human Services.[39] The broadened exemption was added by the House Committee on Ways and Means and accepted by the Senate.[40]

## FEDERAL DISCRIMINATION LAWS

The Civil Rights Act of 1964 makes it an unlawful employment practice for an employer to discriminate against individuals because of their race, color, religion, sex, or national origin. However, the statute also provides that it shall not be an unlawful employment practice for a religious educational institution to hire and employ individuals of a particular religion if the institution is, "in whole or in substantial part," owned by a particular religion or if the curriculum is directed toward the propagation of a particular religion.[41]

Equal Employment Opportunity Commission (EEOC) guidelines in 1967 required employers "to make reasonable accommodations to the religious needs of employees and prospective employees where such accommodation can be made without undue hardship on the conduct of the employer's business."[42] In response to decisions by the Sixth Circuit and the Supreme Court, Congress amended the Civil Rights Act in 1972 by adopting this definition of religion: "The term 'religion' includes all aspects of religious observance and practice, as well as belief, unless an employer demonstrates that he is unable to reasonably accommodate to an employee's

---

[37] Id. (statement by Andrew S. Kinsinger, Chairman, Old Order Amish Steering Committee).
[38] Id. See also the statement by Jesse Neuenschwander, Bishop, Eastern Pennsylvania Mennonite Church, id. at 15.
[39] 102 Stat. 3781-83, § 8007 (1988); 26 U.S.C. § 3127 (2000).
[40] H. Rept. No. 100-795, 100th Cong., 2d Sess. 620 (1988); 134 Cong. Rec. 20497 (1988); H. Rept. No. 100-1104, 100th Cong., 2d Sess. 258-59 (1988).
[41] 78 Stat. 256, § 703(e)(2) (1964).
[42] 29 C.F.R. § 1605.1 (1968).

or prospective employee's religious observance or practice without undue hardship on the conduct of the employer's business."[43]

Litigation has clarified the obligation of employers to accommodate the religious beliefs of employees.[44] The constitutionality of the 1972 legislation reached the Court in 1987. The Mormon Church discharged someone because he was not a member of the Church and not eligible to attend its temples. Although the employee was engaged in nonreligious activities at a nonprofit facility, the Court upheld the 1972 amendment, ruling that any effort by government to distinguish between religious and secular activities would create too much entanglement between church and state.[45]

Open housing legislation in 1968 provided exemptions for religious organizations. Congress prohibited individuals from refusing to sell or rent because of race, color, religion, sex, familial status, or national origin.[46] However, nothing in this general policy prohibits a religious organization from limiting the sale, rental, or occupancy of dwellings that it owns or operates, other than for a commercial purpose, to persons of the same religion, of from giving preferences to such persons, "unless membership in such religion is restricted on account of race, color, or national origin."[47]

## ANIMAL SLAUGHTER

Over the years, states have passed legislation against the inhumane treatment of animals, and many of those laws applied to slaughterhouse operations. Comparable legislation at the national level did not exist until 1958, when Congress passed the Humane Slaughter Act to prevent needless suffering of livestock. Although some companies had improved their procedures, most followed age-old methods: hoisting the animal by a hind leg and moving it to a "sticker," who knifed the jugular vein (not to kill the animal immediately but to cause death by loss of blood), and "knockers" who swung sledgehammers against the animal's head.[48]

In reporting legislation in 1956, the House Committee on Agriculture decided to drop controversial criminal penalties for packers that failed to comply with federal law. As a substitute sanction, the federal government

---

[43] Now codified at 42 U.S.C. § 2000e(j) (2000); see Dewey v. Reynolds Metals Co., 402 U.S. 689 (1971); Dewey v. Reynolds Metals Co., 429 F.2d 324 (6th Cir. 1970).
[44] E.g., Trans World Airlines, Inc. v. Hardison, 432 U.S. 63 (1977).
[45] Corporation of Presiding Bishop v. Amos, 483 U.S. 327 (1987).
[46] 82 Stat. 83, § 804 (1968); 42 U.S.C. § 3604(a) (2000).
[47] 82 Stat. 84, § 807 (1968); 42 U.S.C. § 3607(a) (2000).
[48] 104 Cong. Rec. 1653 (1958).

would refuse to buy meat from any processor who used other than humane methods of slaughtering.[49] When spokesmen for Judaism "expressed concern over the implications of any humane slaughter legislation with respect to the kosher slaughtering of animals,"[50] the committee agreed to make an exception for the Jewish ritualistic method of slaughter. However, many Jewish groups objected to that approach because it seemed to imply that Congress would condemn inhumane slaughtering while tolerating Jewish slaughtering procedures so as not to offend religious freedom. Lawmakers in the House understood their objection and rewrote the bill to make it clear that ritualistic slaughtering is "one of the most humane methods yet devised."[51]

Even with this adjustment, the bill seemed to have little chance of enactment. Officials in the Department of Agriculture claimed there was insufficient knowledge to enable it to determine which methods were humane. They favored the creation of an advisory committee to help study the matter.[52] The meatpacking industry opposed any legislation, preferring to leave the issue in the hands of private industry to devise acceptable slaughtering methods.[53] The Department of the Army, speaking on behalf of the Defense Department, opposed the provision that would prohibit federal agencies from purchasing livestock products unless in compliance with humane slaughtering procedures. The Army was worried that difficulties in satisfying the objectives of the legislation would create shortages in meat supplies.[54]

The Senate Committee on Agriculture and Forestry offered a substitute bill to call for additional research. In surprise move, the committee's substitute proposal failed on a vote of 40 to 43.[55] The House bill then passed the Senate, 72 to 9, after the adoption of some amendments, and the House later agreed to those amendments.[56] The statute specifies two methods of humane slaughter:

> (a) in the case of cattle, calves, horses, mules, sheep, swine, and other livestock, all animals are rendered insensible to pain by a single blow or gunshot or an electrical, chemical or other means that is

---

[49] Id. at 1654.
[50] H. Rept. No. 706, 85th Cong., 1st Sess. 3 (1957).
[51] 104 Cong. Rec. 1654 (1958).
[52] H. Rept. No. 706, 85th Cong., 1st Sess. 3 (1957).
[53] Id.
[54] S. Rept. No. 1724, 85th Cong. 2d Sess. 5 (1958).
[55] 104 Cong. Rec. 15401 (1958).
[56] Id. at 15416-17, 17427.

rapid and effective, before being shackled, hoisted, thrown, cast, or cut; or

(b) by slaughtering in accordance with the ritual requirements of the Jewish faith or any other religious faith that prescribes a method of slaughter whereby the animal suffers loss of consciousness by anemia of the brain caused by the simultaneous and instantaneous severance of the carotid arteries with a sharp instrument.[57]

The legislation provided that nothing in it "shall be construed to prohibit, abridge, or in any way hinder the religious freedom of any person or group." In order to protect freedom of religion, "ritual slaughter and the handling or other preparation of livestock for ritual slaughter are exempted from the terms of this Act." The term "ritual slaughter" is defined in subsection (b) above.[58]

In 1978, Congress amended the statute to toughen the sanctions. Instead of the federal government refusing to purchase livestock products that were not in compliance with the Humane Slaughter Act, the legislation covered all slaughtering conducted under federal and state inspection and all meat or meat food products imported into the United States.[59] The record of the past two decades demonstrated that approximately 90 percent of U.S. plants and foreign plants used humane methods of slaughter.[60]

---

[57] 72 stat. 862, § 2 (1958).
[58] Id. at 864, § 6.
[59] 92 Stat. 1069 (1978); 7 U.S.C. §§ 1901-06 (2000); 21 U.S.C. §§ 603(b), 610(b) (2000).
[60] 124 Cong. Rec. 24580 (1978). See 21 U.S.C. § 464(a) (2000); 9 C.F.R. § 381.11 (1-1-01 ed.).

*Chapter 10*

# CONCLUSIONS

Congress has repeatedly created statutory exemptions to take account of the religious needs of various organizations. As a political body guided primarily by majority vote, it has in fact recognized and given protection to the religious principles of many minority religions. These legislative judgments, balancing the needs of government against the rights of religion, have been upheld in the courts. The process of safeguarding religious liberty depends greatly on the regular political process, driven from the outside by individuals and groups intent on preserving their religious principles. Courts play a role, but not a dominant one.

The United States Code is filled with religious exemptions. On hundreds of occasions, Congress has decided to protect religious interests by exempting them from general laws on taxation, social security, military service, peyote use, discrimination in housing and employment, census questions, rehabilitative services, medical examinations, and public health measures.[1] The basic protection for religious interests comes from this statutory framework. Rather than expect courts to always deliver a remedy, it is healthy to have that task shared with democratic institutions.

Congress typically writes legislative language to accommodate general religious needs. However, there have been occasions when it has identified a particular religious organization (Quakers and Mennonites for conscientious objectors). On other occasions bills have passed Congress that appear to be of a general nature but the legislative history and even much of the statutory language suggest that lawmakers had a particular religious group in mind

---

[1] For the religious exemption on census questions, see 13 U.S.C. §221 (c) (2000); rehabilitation services, 42 U.S.C. § 422(b) (2000); medical examinations, 42 U.S.C. §1396f (2000).

(the Native American Church for the ceremonial use of peyote, the Amish for Social Security, and Orthodox Jews for humane slaughter).

# INDEX

## A

Air Force, 27-30
Alcohol and Drug Abuse Prevention and Treatment (ADAPT), 56
alcoholism, 51, 52
Aleut, 46
alkaloids, 51
America's classrooms, 37
American colonies, 11
American flag, 24
American Indian Defense Association, 42
American Indian Religious Freedom Act (AIRFA), 46, 47, 61
American Indian, 41, 42, 46, 51, 61
Amish, ix, 65, 69-71, 76
amulets, 28
ancestral remains, 49
animal slaughter, 72
antireligious, 34
antislavery, 4
asylums, 66
atheistic, 34

## B

badges, 28
Bald Eagle Protection Act, 44
banned, 42
bearing arms, 11-14, 17
Becker proposal, 36
beer, 68
biblical scriptures, 35
bigamy, 7
Bill of Rights, 3, 12, 24, 53
Black, Justice, 23, 33, 34, 57, 58
blacks, 1, 3, 5, 9
Bradwell, Myra, 5, 6
bread and wine, 51
Brennan, Justice, 29
Brown v. Board of Education, 3, 8
Buchanan, James, 4
Bureau of Indian Affairs (BIA), 43

## C

cemeteries, 66
ceremonial expression, 43
ceremonial use of peyote, 76
charitable, 66
child labor, 8
Chiloquin, Edison, 47, 48
Christian Science, 68
Christianity, 41
Christians, 62, 67
church buildings, 66
church creeds, 17
Church of the Awakening, 55

church-affiliated schools, 66
churches, 16, 55, 65, 66
civil liberties, 8
Civil Rights Act, 5, 9, 45, 71
civil rights, 5, 8, 38, 43, 51
Civil War, 5, 6, 13-15
Cleveland, President Grover, 7
Clinton, President Bill, 39, 44
cohabitation, 7
Collier, John, 42, 43
combatant, 15
Commager, Henry Steele, 8
Commissioner of Indian Affairs, 43
conscientious objector(s), vii, x, 11-19, 65, 75
constitutional amendments, 33, 35-37, 67
constitutional rights, vii, ix, 8, 22, 30, 45
Controlled Substances Act, 55
court-martial, 27
criminal penalties, 50, 72
cultural life, 43

## D

death, 69, 72
Declaration of Independence, 4, 5, 12
deeply spiritual and religious matter, 46
Defense Department, 29, 73
deity, 17, 18, 56
Department of Agriculture, 48, 73
Department of Health, Education, and Welfare, 69
disability, 69
discipline, 28-30
Douglas, Justice, 23, 34, 35
Douglas, Senator Stephen A., 4
Dred Scott v. Sandford, 4
Drug Enforcement Agency (DEA), 55, 61
drug use, 55-58

## E

eagle feathers, 43, 44
Edmunds, Senator George, 7
Eighteenth Amendment, 52, 67, 68
Engel v. Vitale, 33
Equal Access Act, 38
Equal Employment Opportunity Commission (EEOC), 71
Ervin, Jr., Senator Sam J., 34
Eskimo, 46
Establishment Clause, ix, 45, 62, 65
Exemptions from Social Security, 68

## F

face and body paint, 28
failure to salute the flag, 24
Fair Housing Act, 9
farmers, 8, 69
federal courts, 3, 30, 37, 53
Federal Discrimination Laws, 71
federal income tax, 66, 70
federal law, 7, 54, 61, 72
federal regulation, 55, 56
Federal Security Agency, 43
federal statutes, 66
financial risk, 70
First Amendment, 16, 22, 28, 29, 38, 45, 53, 54, 57, 66
flag-salute(s), x, 21, 24
Frankfurter, Justice, 22, 23
Free Exercise Clause, 22, 47, 57-60
freedmen, 14
freedom of worship, 57
funerary/funereal objects, 43, 49, 50

## G

Goldman, Simcha, 27
Goldwater, Senator Barry, 30
government regulation, 68
grace before meals, 39
gravestones, 49

group prayer, 37, 39

## H

habit-forming, 51
Harris, Senator Ira, 13
Hatch, Senator Orrin, 62
Hershey, General Lewis B., 17
high-proof spirits, 68
Hitler, Adolf, 22
Holmes, Jr., Justice Oliver Wendell, 8
homes for the aged, 66
Hopi Indians, 30
Hopi Snake Dance, 42
hospitals, 14, 66
hostile to religion, 34
House Armed Services Committee, 30
House Committee on Interior and Insular Affairs, 45, 46, 49, 50
House Military (Affairs) Committee, 16, 17
House of Representatives, 6, 12
human remains, 49, 50
Humane Slaughter Act, 65, 72, 74
humane slaughter, 73, 76

## I

illegal, 23, 42, 50, 53, 61
In God We Trust, 35
Indian burial grounds, 49
Indian children, 41
Indian Civil Rights Act, 45
Indian culture, 48, 56
Indian dances, 42
Indian funeral ceremonies, 42
Indian graves/tombs, 43, 49
Indian nations, 45, 53
Indian practitioners, 61
Indian religion(s), 41, 43
Indian religious beliefs, vii, x, 41, 42
Indian religious freedom statute, 43

Indian religious leaders, 49
Indian religious practices, 44
Indian religious rights, 41
Indian tribes, 41, 44, 49, 50, 61
Indian uprising, 42
Indians, 31, 41-47, 49, 51, 52, 56, 61, 67
individual liberties, 8, 29
individual rights, 1, 3, 7, 29
ingesting peyote, 51, 56, 57
inhumane treatment of animals, 72
Institute for Government Research, 42
intoxicating liquor(s), 52, 67, 68
intoxicating, 52, 67, 68

## J

Jackson, Justice, 24
Jackson, Rep. James, 12, 13
Jackson, Robert H., 24
Jehovah's Witnesses, 21, 23, 24
Jewish male, 27
Jewish Seder, 68
Jewish slaughtering, 73
Johnson, Lyndon B., 43
Johnson, President Andrew, 5
joining in prayer, 35
Judeo-Christian religions, 61
judicial record, vii, ix, 8, 9
jugular vein, 72
Justice Department, 23, 24, 29, 55

## K

Kennedy, President John F., 43
Klamath Indian Lands, 48
Klamath Indian nation, 47
Klamath Indian(s), 43, 47-49, 56
kosher slaughtering, 73

## L

Lincoln Administration, 14

Lincoln, Abraham, 4
livestock, 73, 74
loss of blood, 72

## M

Madison, James, 3, 12, 13
Maine Constitution, 12
male workforce, 70
Marshall, Justice, 29
Medical Corps, 15
Mennonites, ix, 14, 75
Meriam, Lewis, 42
mescaline, 51, 54, 55, 58
military duties, 29, 30, 31
military service, 12, 14, 15, 30, 75
militia, 11, 12, 13
minister of a church, 68
minorities, 1, 3, 6, 7, 22
minority political groups, 8
minority religions, 75
minority rights, vii, ix, 1, 3, 8, 25
missionary societies, 66
moment of silence, 37
Mormon Church, 6, 7, 60, 72
Mormons, 6, 7
Murphy, Justice, 7, 23, 24
Muslims, 30

## N

National Association of Evangelicals, 60
National Defense Act, 15
National Museum of the American Indian, 49
national origin, 71, 72
Native American Church (NAC), ix, 45, 51, 53-59, 76
Native American culture, 44
Native American religious practices, 44
Native Hawaiians, 46
Navajo country, 53

Navajo Tribal Council, 45, 53
Navajos, 53
Negro children, 9
New Hampshire Constitution, 12
New Mexico, 45, 51, 53
Nixon, Richard, 43
noncombatant, 11, 14, 15, 17
non-Indian religious body, 55
Non-Indian religious missions, 41

## O

O'Connor, Justice, 47
object of worship, 51
obsolete laws, 43
Office of Indian Affairs, 42
Office of Legal Counsel (OLC), 55
old age, 69
Old Amish Order/Old Order Amish, 69, 70
Oregon Supreme Court, 57, 58
orphanages, 66
orthodox belief, 18
Orthodox Jew(s), 27, 28, 76

## P

parsonages, 66
People v. Woody, 53
peyote, 51-61, 75
places of worship, 66
pledging allegiance to the flag, 24
political process, ix, 1, 3, 9, 41, 75
polygamy, 6, 7
poorhouses, 66
possession of peyote, 57
prayer clubs, 39
prayers in public schools, 35
property taxes, 66
public schools, 33-35, 37, 39
Pueblo de Taos Indians, 45

## Q

Quaker(s), ix, 11, 12, 13, 14, 16, 75
Quartermaster Corps, 15

## R

rabbi, 27
race, 5, 71, 72
Reagan, President Ronald, 37
recite the prayer, 33, 35
religion, ix, 16, 17, 22, 29, 34, 36, 39, 41, 43-47, 53, 57, 60, 61, 65, 66, 69, 71, 72, 74, 75
religious activities, 38, 39
religious and civil liberties, 60, 62
religious apparel, vii, x, 30, 31, 65
religious beliefs, 7, 21, 22, 24, 41, 54, 71, 72
religious ceremon(y)ies, 51, 53-57, 61, 67
religious community, 70
religious denominations, vii, ix, 13, 14, 15
religious dietary laws, 65
religious educational institution, 71
religious exemptions, 13, 57, 65, 75
religious expression, 39
religious faith, 31, 53, 74
Religious Freedom Restoration Act (RFRA), 59-62
religious freedom, ix, 1, 24, 27, 30, 43, 46, 47, 56, 59-61, 73, 74
religious groups, 9, 19, 37, 38, 59, 62
religious headgear, 29
religious liberties, ix, 1, 3
Religious Liberty Protection Act (RLPA), 62
religious liberty, vii, ix, x, 1, 3, 6, 9, 21, 23, 25, 27, 33, 45, 47, 57, 60, 75
religious minorities, vii, ix, 34
religious objections, 11, 21
religious observance, 71

religious opinion, 57
religious order, 68
religious orders, 68
religious organizations, ix, 11, 15, 16, 21, 22, 36, 59, 63, 65, 66, 72
religious practice(s), 7, 41, 46, 53, 54, 59
religious principles, 11, 68, 75
religious sect, 12, 15, 16, 68
Religious Society of Friends, 16
religious struggle, 9
religious training, 16, 17, 18, 19
religious use of peyote, x, 55, 57, 58, 61, 65
retirement, 69
right of citizenship, 5
rings, 28
ritual slaughter, 74
ritualistic method of slaughter, 73
robes, 28
Roosevelt, President Franklin D., 8
Rutledge, Wiley, 23, 24

## S

sacrament, 51, 53, 61
sacramental purposes, 53, 56, 67, 68
sacramental wines, 67
sacrilegious, 34
school prayer, vii, x, 36, 37
school prayers, 36, 37
Second Amendment, 13
secondary schools, 38
Secretary of Defense, 28
Secretary of the Air Force, 28
Secretary of the Interior, 44, 50
secular symbol, 21
segregation, 3
selective service, 11, 15, 16, 17
Selective Training and Service Act, 16
self-employed, 69, 70
Senate Armed Services Committee, 30

Senate Committee on Indian Affairs, 61
Senate Judiciary Committee, 8, 35, 37, 60, 62
Senate Military Affairs Committee, 16
Seventh-Day Adventists, 17
sex discrimination, 9
sex, 6, 9, 71, 72
sexual excess, 42
Sherbert v. Verner, 57
skullcap, 27, 29
slavery, 4, 14, 15
slaves, 4, 8, 11, 14
Smith, Alfred, 56
Smithsonian Institution, 49
Social Security tax(es), 65, 69
Social Security, 65, 68-71, 76
soldiers, 13, 14, 15
speech, 8, 38
spineless cactus, 51
spiritual beliefs, 48
statutory exemptions, vii, x, 65, 75
Stevens, Justice, 28, 70
students, 33, 36, 38, 39
suffering of livestock, 72
Sun Dance, 42
Supreme Being, 17, 18, 19, 54
symbolic daggers, 28

## T

Taos Indians, 45
Taos Pueblo Indians, 46
Taos religious shrines, 43, 45
tax exemptions, 65, 66
tax system, 8
The Meriam Report, 42
traditional definition of religion, 18
traditional values, 48
tribal laws, 53
tribal religious ceremonies, 44
turbans, 28, 30

## U

unemployment, 56, 57, 58, 59, 69

## V

Vermont Constitution, 12
voluntary prayer, 35, 37
volunteers, 13, 70
Voting Rights Act, 9
voting rights, 7

## W

war dance, 42
Webb-Kenyon Act, 67
Wilson, President Woodrow, 15
wine, 65, 67, 68
Winema National Forest, 47, 48
women, 1, 3, 5, 6, 9, 70
World War I, 15, 17, 68
World War II, 16, 23
Wounded Knee, 42
Wyoming, 51

## Y

yarmulke, 27-29